Boris Karloff poses for a casual IMHOTEP portrait with artist Ray Jones.

MIDNIGHT MARQUEE #81

Editor
Gary J. Svehla

Graphic Design Interior
Gary J. Svehla

Front/Back Cover
Aurelia Susan Svehla

Copy Editor
Janet Atkinson
Aurelia Susan Svehla

Writers
Barry Atkinson
Christopher Gullo
Gregory Mank
Don Mankowski
Jim Nemeth
Ray and Gail Orwig
Gary J. Svehla

Special Thanks!
Beth Cox at McFarland; Richard Klemensen; Ben Ohmart of BearManor Media; David Colton and the CHFB; David "Charlie" Ellis; George Stover; Carlo Wittig; Aurelia Susan Svehla; and all the writers who vehemently supported the effort.

Publisher
Midnight Marquee Press, Inc.

ISBN 978-1-64430-132-6
LOC 2022946842

Gary J. Svehla and Aurelia Susan Svehla, Midnight Marquee #81, October 2022, copyright ©2022 by Gary J. Svehla, 9721 Britinay Ln, Parkville, MD 21234; phone: 410-665-1198, website: www.midmar.com; e-mail: midmargary@aol.com; Available from Amazon.com and any place that sells books.

ARTICLES for issue 82, our 60th anniversary issue, are due Jan. 15, 2023. I want the issue to be a regular issue and not a tribute issue. Our focus has been on Classic Horror from the 1930s—1970s and generally we are not interested in newer movies unless they connect to Classic Horror. The article should be sent as a WORD or compatible file, single-spaced with no formatting (no headers or footers, no page numbers, etc.). Feel free to discuss article ideas via e-mail. First time writers are welcome, but veteran writers are always appreciated. 4 to 6 pages is a decent length but longer articles are welcomed as well.

Playing at the Midnight Marquee

When my wife Sue was telling potential writers that this would be the final issue of *Midnight Marquee*, I was thinking, "Would this really be?" I am about to turn 73 and I clearly remember back on January 9, 2020 when I had a stroke. I have been recovering ever since. Well, let's just say this may have been the final issue. But then I thought, next year the mag will be 60! Sixty years I've been doing Midmar. So we have to do at least one more issue to celebrate that momentous anniversary.

Others have not been as lucky as me. Take for example David Robinson, designer of the front and back cover of last issue #80, who succumbed to cancer. I can remember when I first approached the Robinson brothers in the early 1970s to do art for my magazine and now, 50 years later, one of them is gone. Mark, God bless you on your journey alone, and keep the artwork coming.

Then Dave Metzler, co-creator of the original first few issues of *Gore Creatures*, died suddenly in a rather unusual way. He was feeling rather unwell while working one Friday at his Washington-based CPA company, and he decided to go home to rest. His employees were extremely worried when he failed to show up for work the following Monday. When he didn't answer his phone they had someone check his home and he was found to have died from a blood clot that traveled to his heart.

After my stroke, it was difficult to return to work on the books and magazines. I was reduced to being a one finger typist, since the last two fingers of my right hand were curled down and the first two fingers, although straight, were slow to bend, it was easier to use the index finger of my left hand to hunt and peck, although my doctor advised me to try to use both hands to type. I would accidentally highlight portions of manuscripts and delete text to the degree that one of our writers suggested that it might be time to retire. But eventually, over time, this problem and others gradually corrected themselves and I am back to my almost usual or should I say unusual self. I am much slower doing the books, but I eventually get the job done.

Things have changed a lot since the last issue, namely COVID-19, which has made the world a smaller place. Mask-wearing and social distancing have become the norm. Staying isolated at home and avoiding social interaction is a necessity, although we take our chances interacting with close friends. We never go to the movies anymore but watch films in our home theater, our one indulgence in life. During all this duress, Sue and I have been trying to figure how to transform our 3-level split into a one level living area so we can age gracefully in place, as they say. Senior communities are very attractive but are way beyond the range of most middle-class families. So, we continue trying to find a solution.

Since this magazine was formed in 1963 (can it be 59 years ago?), it becomes increasingly more challenging to find new things to write about 90-year-old movies, and even more recent ones. The competition is greater than ever before, and it is so hard to remain relevant in today's over-crowded magazine market. Even *Monsters from The Vault* must find it daunting to get that final issue out in an ever-changing environment where magazines come, go, and are quickly forgotten. Even Classic Horror Film Board guru David Colton asks in his webpages if *Famous Monsters of Filmland* is really gone for good?

Yet my closest ally in fandom, Richard Klemensen, still carries on the British torch after nearing 50 years of publishing, but he has announced that issue #51, to be published when he is 78 years old, will be his final issue. *Classic Monsters of the Movies* manages to carry on and sell out of each new issue. The articles might not have a lot new to say, but the graphic design is really nice to look at.

It is interesting, if not satisfying, to remember the saying: "He that is first will sooner be last." I remember when *Mid-*

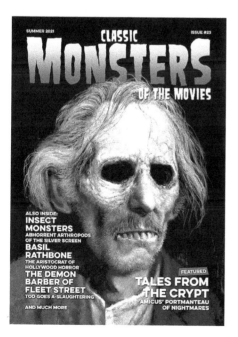

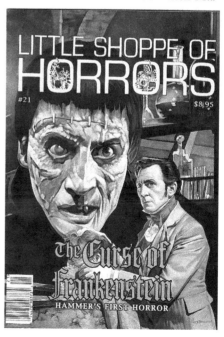

COLUMBIA PICTURES present

DANA ANDREWS
PEGGY CUMMINS
and NIALL MacGINNIS

Chosen...singled out to die...victim of his imagination or victim of a demon?

Night of the Demon

Screenplay by CHARLES BENNETT and HAL E. CHESTER
Based on the Story "Casting the Runes" by Montague R. James
Directed by JACQUES TOURNEUR • Produced by FRANK BEVIS

Executive Producer HAL E. CHESTER
A SABRE FILM Production

Lon Chaney shall not die!

night Marquee was right up there with the big boys of the 1960s and 1970s, but now, we are slowly being forgotten by the slew of new, small-press publications. That is not so bad, as I know we influenced the current horde of genre magazines. They might not even know our name, but we influenced them nonetheless. The torch has been passed to younger fans who are exploring horror fandom for a new generation. Let's face it, monster fandom will find it difficult to be as big today as it once was back in the 1950s and 1960s.

Where are *Shock Theatre*, Zacherley, Forrest J Ackerman, Aurora monster model kits, monster bubble gum cards, et al.? Of course today we have garage monster model kits, a slew of new TV and web horror hosts, modern monster publications, horror websites and horror conventions (but forgive me if I still think none are as good as FANEX). So, horror fandom might not be in such as bad shape a as we may think. It is simply different and caters to more current film fare. Classic films from the '30s and '40s will soon be 100 years old. The first *Star Wars* released in 1977 is considered quaint and foreign films are readily available and rival American productions. My fear is that Hammer films from the '50s and '60s will replace Universal horror, which might soon be forgotten. I remember Forrest J Ackerman's rallying cry, "Lon Chaney shall not die," but when all the people who remember Chaney, Sr. are gone, who will be left to honor him?

While newer magazines are trying to say different things about the old chestnuts, all the classic and not-so-classic horror films are being released for the fifth or sixth time (videotape, DVD, Laserdisc, Blu Ray disc, 4k disc and we can't neglect streaming). We can either decide that we cannot see the difference in resolution or buy the latest version of *Frankenstein*, which becomes less and less special with each new release. It just isn't the same when you can grab every conceivable movie off the shelf, movies we could only dream about as kids. We grew up in the generation that had to wait to see a favor-

ite film when it appeared theatrically or showed up randomly on television.

We can't even begin to mourn the loss of so many horror film icons since the last issue—there have been so many of them, including a special friend Veronica Carlson. But most of all we feel the loss of icon Christopher Lee, which completed the procession of Lon Chaney, Bela Lugosi, Boris Karloff, Lon Chaney, Jr., Peter Cushing and now Christopher Lee. And what is so sad is that the list of greats stops here. There will be horror film actors, but never horror film icons. The list ended with Christopher Lee.

So, for example, take a classic horror movie such as *Night of the Demon* and think of all the approaches at film criticism: you have the "making of" production history, you have interviews with the cast and crew, you have personal criticism, you have film comparisons, you have star and crew remembrances, you have author remembrances and often disdain for the project. Then you may have comparisons to films in a series or remakes. You may have current "hot licks" sexual analysis or ranting how a specific film hates women … or men or gays. You might have political or social metaphoric appraisals of the film. And all this plus more has been covered again and again. The passion to restate the obvious is based upon one's love or hatred of the movie and can be satisfied by watching the same movie every few years or simply ignoring it. But haven't most films been covered to death? Perhaps personal criticism is the only thing left to explore, as every writer has his or her opinion—hopefully giving readers a fresh new way to watch the film. If we have 1,000 people who desire to write on one specific film, we have 1,000 different ways of perceiving that one film.

Even if, due to unforeseen circumstances, this is the final issue, I say write on! Be the 1,000th person trying to say something new about something old. That is your challenge. But thankfully there are new horror films made all the time, but don't dare to forget the old ones and the shoulders the new ones stand upon. Remember Karloff and Lugosi, James Whale, Carl Laemmle, Terence Fisher, Freddie Francis, Peter Cushing, Christopher Lee, Anthony Hinds, Michael Carreras, Mario Bava, Dario Argento and Sam Raimi. Remember all the classic films we still love, and study the modern horror films and those yet to come.

Hopefully, see you all next issue.

—Gary J. Svehla

By Barry Atkinson

THE RETURN OF THE VAMPIRE
BELA LUGOSI'S FINEST HOUR AS AN UNDEAD COUNT

"This is the case of Armand Tesla, vampire, as compiled from the personal notes of Professor Walter Saunders, King's College, Oxford. The following events took place in the outskirts of London towards the close of the year 1918. They began on the night of October the 15th, a particularly gloomy, foggy night that was well suited for a visitation by the supernatural." So goes the splendid opening narration to Columbia's *The Return of the Vampire*, spoken over Lew Landers' panning camera that slowly glides around Priory Cemetery, dense mist swirling, the shriek of a screech owl piercing the gloom, a raven perched on a twisted bough, someone furtively prowling among the overgrown gravestones and leaning crosses, heightening the atmosphere of dread. As the narration ends, Landers closes in on the prowler's face, a werewolf on the alert, a row of gleaming sharp teeth and fangs bared, there at the bidding of his vampire master, 200-year-old Romanian Count

Armand Tesla. The wolf man descends into a cobwebby crypt, pausing at a coffin. "Master, it's night again," he whispers. "Beautiful, dark, silent night, with the fog creeping in. Time for you to awaken, Master. Time for you to go out." The coffin lid creaks open, a ringed hand emerges from the plush lining and the wolf man stares at his Master's shadow looming on the

Buenas noches, Lady Ainsley.

Bela Lugosi approaches Lady Jane Ainsley (Frieda Inescort) while she plays the piano.

wall, dogs howling in distress. "Andreas. You will tell me what has transpired during the hours of light," is the command, the wolf man informing the vampire that his latest victim lies comatose in Dr. Ainsley's Sanatorium. To a chorus of yelping, barking dogs, the bloodsucker exits the crypt and walks through the fog, rearing up like a giant bat and disappearing into the mist, ironically in front of a tilted wooden cross. Similar to the opening scene in *Frankenstein Meets the Wolf Man*, this four-minute sequence ranks as one of the 1940s finest of all horror audience grabbers, orchestrated with a genuine feel for the genre. Yes, in this reviewer's estimation, Columbia's 1943 vampire opus is right up there with the best of what Universal was knocking out during that period and, bucking convention, I'll state right here and now that Bela Lugosi is on far more formidable form here than he was in *Dracula*, made 12 years earlier. Out of the two, give me *The Return of the Vampire* any day of the week; ahead of its time, the pic-

Matt Willis' werewolf makeup by Clay Campbell is often described as cute, but it scared the girls back in 1962.

Andreas is the slave to Armand Tesla (Bela Lugosi) and a threat to ladies anywhere.

ture is similar to a horror film conceived in the 1950s rather than the 1940s, Lugosi commanding and mesmerizing in the last of his big-budget productions where he would receive top billing; the added (and novel) attraction of Matt Willis playing his reluctant werewolf assistant, Andreas Obry, is a definite bonus for fans of this type of horror fare.

Columbia envisaged *The Return of the Vampire* as a follow-up to Universal's *Dracula*, but as soon as Universal's lawyers heard about their plans, the company was threatened with a lawsuit for plagiarism. Dracula, therefore, became Armand Tesla, and 60-year-old Lugosi, who was freelancing at the time, was hired for the lead role which he fit in between work on his Monogram potboilers (seven completed, two more to finish)—his fee $3,500 for four week's work, August 21 through to mid-September 1943. Unlike the Poverty Row Monograms, Columbia's vampire feature was deemed an "A" production, budgeted at $75,000, the film eventually raking in over a million dollars after repeated screenings in the US and England. It was shown continually in the late '50s/early'60s, usually teamed with Mid Century's British X-rated 1959 shocker *Jack the Ripper*. The US release date was held back for November 11, 1943, so as not to clash with Universal's *Son of Dracula*, released on November 5. After the end of WWII, the British Censor's office awarded the movie an "H" certificate in early 1946 (horror films were deemed unsuitable for the shell-shocked public during the war and were mostly banned) following around two minutes of minor

cuts, including the scene at the end where Lugosi melts under the sun's rays; these edits were reinstated in the 1950s when the picture was re-classified an "X" and restored to the original running length of 69 minutes.

Jack Pierce's Lon Chaney wolf man design from the Universal flicks was off limits, so Clay Campbell, Columbia's main makeup artist, was called upon to come up with a Matt Willis werewolf creation every bit as good, and, to his credit, made a decent job of it; moreover, Willis' wolf man is onscreen a great deal more than Chaney was in his five Wolf Man features. Campbell was the man responsible for the she-wolf and wolf man in 1952's *Jungle Jim in the Forbidden Land* (also directed by Landers) and, more notably, Steven Ritch's agonized lycanthrope in *The Werewolf* (1956). Some maintain that Willis' makeup job is more cute than scary ("Like a Yorkshire terrier," joked one wag), but all I know is that when I caught the film in July 1962, there were more than a few screams from the female members of the audience when the actor's hairy face loomed into full-screen fright mode in a packed auditorium, so, in that respect, it must have been effective; and how many other movies could boast a vampire count *and* a talkative werewolf right-hand man who both shared equal billing? On the composing front, Italian Mario Castelnuovo-Tedesco conjured up a fantastic, richly textured ominous score to rival those written by Universal's Hans J. Salter, while Griffin Jay and Randall Faye's screenplay, taken from an idea put forward by Kurt Neumann, laid on the tangled intrigue with aplomb. And the moody black-and-white photography, courtesy of L. William O'Connell (he worked on Howard Hawks' 1932 *Scarface*) and John Stumar, was truly outstanding, shrouding the sets in shadowy hues, complementing Landers' efficient direction.

In a publicity photo Bela Lugosi tries to put the bite on lovely Nicki (Nina Foch).

It's the combination of all these elements, a pooling of little-known talents (apart, of course, for Lugosi), that gives *The Return of the Vampire* its extra bite (excuse the pun) over the opposition, making it a far grittier, full-blooded proposition than the rather wishy-washy antics prevalent in, say, *Dracula's Daughter* (1936) and *Son of Dracula*, both granted the less restrictive British "A" certificate. The precredits shot of a terrified woman backing against a wall and screaming her head off as a cloaked figure approaches her in the darkness ("The imagination of man at times sires the fantastic and the grotesque. That the imagination of man can soar into the stratosphere of fantasy is attested by—," The RETURN OF THE VAMPIRE are the words overlaying this brief scene; some prints omit this, displaying only the main title) plus that afore-mentioned creepy cemetery opener, guaranteed an adult "H" classification in Britain—and that's before we got into the narrative proper!

At the Ainsley Sanatorium, Professor Walter Saunders (Gilbert Emery) and Lady Jane Ainsley (Frieda Inescort) are puzzling over a female patient's bloodless condition, thinking it a severe case of anemia and noticing two odd puncture wounds on her throat. The woman mutters, "Eyes like burning coals. They're hurting me," before suddenly dying from shock. At just gone midnight, Saunders reads a journal written by one Dr. Armand Tesla, an authority on vampires, the academic stating that the creature is "a monster. A fantastic something that draws blood from the human body through the jugular veins of its victims."

Could those marks on the dead woman's throat have been made by a vampire? Upstairs, Saunders' young granddaughter Nicki is visited in her bedroom by Tesla; the French windows fling wide, mist streams into the room, the wind moans, leaves blow across the floor and a shadow appears on the wall, the little girl screaming as she's enveloped by that bat-like shadow, a highly atmospheric scene charged with eerie menace. In the morning, Nicki cannot be woken and exhibits bite marks on her neck. Time for action! "You're really convinced that Nicki was attacked by a vampire?" an incredulous Lady Jane asks the Professor before the two decide to visit the long-abandoned Priory burial ground, Saunders armed with an axe and long metal spike. Spotting queer footprints in the dirt, they follow the prints into the vampire's sunless crypt, unaware that Andreas, in werewolf mode, is lurking among the tombstones, wondering what is going on. "It's a man! But he's alive!" Lady Jane breathes hard in alarm when they open the coffin. To prove that the unholy being lying in its resting place is a member of the undead, Saunders produces a mirror, holding it up to the body's face; it shows no reflection, only the clothing. Banging the spike into Tesla's heart, there's a deep groan and outside, Andreas, his master gone, changes from werewolf to human, the curse lifted—for now.

Twenty-three years later, during the early days of the Second World War, Chief Commissioner for Scotland Yard, Sir Frederick Fleet (Miles Mander), is browsing through Professor Saunders' manuscript on "The Case of Armand Tesla who died in 1744 and became a vampire." Saunders expired in a plane

Armand Tesla (Bela Lugosi) is hot for blood as he eyes a victim laying prone on the stone tomb.

Master and slave

crash (caused by Tesla's curse) so is not around to pour water on Sir Frederick's scepticism on the subject. Tesla's "Man Friday," Andreas, now works for Lady Jane in her laboratory, the aristocrat under threat of prosecution for the murder of Tesla, the detective refusing to give credence to the fact that he might have been a vampire, dismissing such ideas as pure fantasy. Music conductor John Ainsley (Roland Varno) turns up to add just a spot of romance (but not that much) to this macabre tale; he's engaged to Nicki (Nina Foch). Lady Jane suggests opening Tesla's grave ("The body will not be decomposed."), but during an air raid the old cemetery is bombed. Two civil defense workmen engaged in clearing up the wreckage spot Tesla's corpse, yank out the spike, or "bomb splinter," (there's a prolonged sigh, probably of relief) and put the coffin "in a hole." Andreas, unaware of this, doesn't want Sir Frederick to reopen the tomb, afraid that Tesla will rise again; he has no desire to become the Count's unwilling henchman for a second time. But his former master has returned full of vengeance; hands scrabbling away the dirt, dogs howling in terror at his vile presence, the vampire calls upon Andreas to assist him in his devilish work. The two meet in the foggy cemetery: "You have no power over me. I'm no longer your

slave. Lady Ainsley has cleansed me of your evil. You can't bring it back," Andreas challenges Tesla, but the vampire's deep-set eyes bore into him and Andreas quickly transforms into his werewolf state. "Master. You have come back." Andreas now looks almost pleased at seeing the vampire again. "I must find a new resting place. There you will bring the coffin with my native soil. Then I have other plans," Tesla announces with relish, locating a crypt beneath the bomb-blasted ruins of St. Mathias Church in London. On the loose again, Tesla takes on the guise of Dr. Hugo Bruckner, a German scientist who escaped from a Nazi concentration camp but was murdered by Andreas (it's Bruckner's belongings that are in that parcel that Andreas carries around with him) and sets about plotting his revenge on Lady Jane and her family; he wants Nicki to join him as one of the undead. Infiltrating John and Nicki's engagement party on a charm offensive, he instructs Andreas to steal Saunders' manuscript and stalks the streets at night for victims, homing in on Nicki; her room is drenched in black misty shadows as the vampire calls to her: "Nicki. I'm waiting for you. Come to me. Come. It is useless to struggle." She walks downstairs, confronting Tesla in a fog-shrouded room, hypnotized by his magnetic eyes. "Look at me, Nicki.

Bela Lugosi, famous star of RETURN OF THE VAMPIRE.

Now tell me who I am. I am Tesla," he leers in true Lugosi style, piling on the dramatics in his trademark thick Hungarian accent. "And I can never die. And you are mine. Forever! Your mind is no longer your own. I shall command and you shall obey!" There follows a brief, very murky shot, of Andreas the wolf man watching his master clamber into his coffin (cut from British prints in the '40s) and then Nicki is receiving a blood transfusion, two punctures clearly visible on her neck.

Tesla's ring is recovered by Lady Jane after she's interviewed the two workmen ("We pulled the spike out. We 'eard a sorta gasp. We buried him again, ma'am."), relaying details of the conversation to Sir Frederick; however, he scoffs at her no-tions of a vampire at large. "Rubbish, my dear lady. I will not believe in galloping ghosts." But, to be on the safe side, he has Andreas tailed by two officers who struggle violently with him in an alley; Andreas reverts to his fierce werewolf alter ego, the policeman horrified but managing to seize his parcel as he escapes. At the office, the contents indicate that they once belonged to Bruckner, the cops claiming that they were attacked by a wolf, not a man ("He turned into a wolf, Sir, right in front of our eyes!"). To prove it, they produce a bunch of hair; Sir Frederick is amazed to discover that the strands match those of the hair found on the broken drawer where Saunders' manuscript was pinched.

In Nicki's bedroom, werewolf Andreas, staring through the window, sneaks in and grabs her maid; Nicki, a bandage wound around her neck, arises. Downstairs, she vampirizes fiancé John, Sir Frederick later grilling Dr. Bruckner/ Tesla at John's bedside. "There are many strange things in the world, Sir Frederick. Vampires may be one of them," answers Tesla slyly. Andreas is the next to be questioned by Lady Jane and the detective. "Did you take the manuscript? What were you doing outside the Professional Club at three o'clock this morning? Let me see your hands!" Unfortunately, Andreas' left hand is covered in fur. "He's still under the domination of Tesla," says Lady Jane as Andreas, admitting to the theft of Saunders' journal, leaps out of a window, refusing to reveal the whereabouts of the vampire: "You can never destroy the Master. He'll live forever!" is his dramatic parting shot.

At Bruckner's club, Sir Frederick knows that, from records in his possession, this specific Bruckner bears no resemblance to the real Bruckner; in the fake Bruckner's room, all the mirrors have been turned to the wall and a ring is found. "Dr. Bruckner is Armand Tesla, vampire, whose face casts no reflection," Lady Jane states emphatically to Sir Frederick, two plainclothes detectives on the door failing to see Bruckner/Tesla who, using his vampiric powers, eludes the pair, leaving the building undetected.

Lady Jane now prepares to trap the bloodsucker and give him a taste of his own medicine. As she plays the organ, Tesla appears. "What a fool you are. A fool. Tonight, I will take Nicki. Tonight."

"You are evil," she shouts, uncovering a glowing cross on the organ.

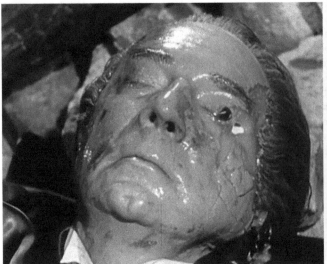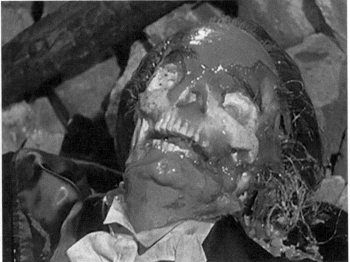

(left) The beginning of Bela Lugosi's melting death; (right) Tesla's melting death continues.

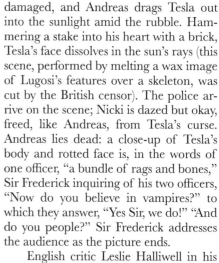

The Return of The Vampire, **if produced by Universal, would have garnered far more recognition than it does today.**

With a yell, Tesla leaps back and disappears in a clap of thunder. But he hasn't given up on his main quarry. In Nicki's bedroom, the windows open, leaves rustle across the floor, the wind whistles around the room, Tesla's voice coming from afar: "Follow my voice. Nothing can keep you from me." She wanders downstairs in a trance, Sir Frederick and Lady Jane observing her and concerned for her welfare, deciding to see where she is heading. Off through the gates into the foggy night she drifts in her white nightgown, akin to a vampire bride, gnarled trees and crosses protruding through the billowing mist as she enters the cemetery, a keening wind backed by baying dogs, Tedesco's evocative music rising to a crescendo, a wonderfully tense and atmospheric few minutes of '40s horror cinema; the lighting effects are genuinely superb. "The night is our friend, Nicki. Closer, Nicki. Closer. And we will be together. Just you and I. Together." Tesla stands there like a satanic statue, his hairy acolyte hovering in the shadows; sirens wail to warn of a bombing raid, Sir Frederick shoots at Andreas, bombs drop and the wolf man, mortally wounded, picks up Nicki, taking her to the ruined church and placing her unconscious on a slab.

Turning to Tesla, he pleads with him: "Help me, Master. You promised me eternal life, like yours. Forever." The vampire savagely turns

on him, sneering. "I no longer need you, Andreas. Your usefulness is over. Get away from me. Idiot. Get back to that corner. Remain there to die." Yes, if ever anyone sympathized with the plight of a werewolf in a horror movie, it's poor old Andreas Obry in this one. As Tesla gloats over Nicki's still form ("There is no power great enough to keep you from me. I have won."), Andreas scrabbles in the dirt and uncovers a crucifix. Changing back into human form, the words of Lady Jane echo in his head: "Goodness is the strongest force in the world." Andreas forces Tesla back across the crypt with the cross. "You are my master no longer. You're evil. You must be destroyed. For years I've lived in terror of you, waking up screaming. I'm going to destroy you forever." Another blitz gets underway, the building is badly

damaged, and Andreas drags Tesla out into the sunlight amid the rubble. Hammering a stake into his heart with a brick, Tesla's face dissolves in the sun's rays (this scene, performed by melting a wax image of Lugosi's features over a skeleton, was cut by the British censor). The police arrive on the scene; Nicki is dazed but okay, freed, like Andreas, from Tesla's curse. Andreas lies dead: a close-up of Tesla's body and rotted face is, in the words of one officer, "a bundle of rags and bones," Sir Frederick inquiring of his two officers, "Now do you believe in vampires?" to which they answer, "Yes Sir, we do!" "And do you people?" Sir Frederick addresses the audience as the picture ends.

English critic Leslie Halliwell in his yearly *Film Guide* commented that the movie was a "surprisingly well made and complexly plotted horror film; it looks good and only lacks humor," praise indeed from a man who was known to treat most vintage horror pictures with a certain amount of disdain. The review is tempered with "The wolf man, however, is a regrettable intrusion," not a sentiment the majority of film buffs would go along with. Made by all concerned with a high degree of care and professionalism combined with a bona fide love of their craft, *The Return of the Vampire*, if produced by Universal, would have garnered far more recognition than it does today. As it is, there is no doubt that the movie successfully punches above its weight, knocking into a cocked hat many of Universal's lesser horror output of the '30s and '40s. Was it a case of Columbia executives getting their heads together and thinking, "Anything Universal can do, we can also do, and in this case, do better." It also demonstrated that, in his chosen milieu, Bela Lugosi at that time had very few equals. By turns charismatic, sinister and, arrogant, Lugosi's Count Armand Tesla is alongside Count Dracula as one of cinema's all-time greatest vampires. Lew Landers' vampire outing, like a fine wine, improves with age, possessing a real archaic charm that viewers can revel in on repeated viewings; simply put, it looks the business. And Matt Willis' tragically memorable Andreas represents a wolf man with a tortured soul that we can all pin one's faith in and feel sorry for, a rarity indeed in the realm of horror cinema.

TERRIFYING! PARALYZING! HORRIFYING!

The RETURN of the VAMPIRE

BELA LUGOSI

with FRIEDA INESCORT • NINA FOCH • MILES MANDER

SCREEN PLAY BY GRIFFIN JAY

Directed by LEW LANDERS • Produced by SAM WHITE

A COLUMBIA PICTURE

THE BLACK ROOM
BORIS KARLOFF AS VICTIM AND VILLAIN

BY NATHALIE YAFET

It wasn't easy growing up being the only girl who loved monsters in Oconomowoc, Wisconsin. The only way to get the horror magazines was either at the taxi stand or bus station, both officially deemed "occasions of sin" by the nuns in school. The businesses earned that dubious status by selling other sketchier titles. I hadn't figured out the subscription angle yet, so I bought my *Famous Monsters* at one of those places. Then other zines began to appear. One of the more interesting ones was *Modern Monsters* from Prestige Publications, which lasted only four issues. A regular feature was "Shock Theater!" with capsule descriptions of selected films and photos. Issue four had *The Black Room* written up, a new-to-me Karloff film. The reviewer gets Anton and Gregor mixed up, calls Thea "Marian" (the name of the actress) and is vague about the actual black room in the movie, but I didn't know any better and fixated on seeing it. My only source for horror movies was *Nightmare Theater* on WITI Channel 6 Milwaukee. Its genial and loopy host, Dr. Cadaverino, hadn't

shown it yet and our black-and-white TV had no UHF antenna, which would have been my portal to the real *Shock Theater*. Coming up empty on the usual sources— even the sacred *Famous Monsters* hadn't covered it in my limited experience. I

Boris Karloff, Von and the corpse of Marian Marsh

despaired of ever seeing or even knowing more about it.

When the rest of my six-person family was asleep as I should have been, I would try to tune in stations beyond the VHF range. This never worked but I kept trying with it. One snowy night something was there. Fuzzy picture but intact, decent sound. A wedding was stopped by a dog rushing the altar (the *Modern Monsters* review said, "His marriage to fair Marian (should have been the character name, Thea) is halted and hounded by the family dog." This had to be *The Black Room*! The movie continued with the dog (Thor played by Von) chasing Gregor in his carriage back to the castle and excitingly pushing him down into the pit, onto dead Anton's knife. I never did find out exactly which station I managed to catch as the picture and sound went out right after the movie ended, but it was most probably WGN channel 9, Chicago, Illinois.

I waited 20 years until I finally saw the whole movie on VHS. Since that date I've added two DVD copies, an eight-millimeter Castle Films reel, a laserdisc

The twin brothers: [left] the evil Gregor and [right] the benevolent Anton

and every category of movie paper and memorabilia that I could get (which very unfortunately does not currently include a one sheet or an insert from the original 1935 release.)

Some years ago, I had the opportunity to speak with Marian Marsh on the phone, courtesy of Greg Mank, who offered me her contact information. The kind gesture came with a warning that I could never get her to sign and return stills, since others had tried and never succeeded. The conversation was unforgettable. Ms. Marsh charmingly related the story of Boris' pet pig, Violet, who lived in a playpen in the Karloff home. And she enthusiastically told me how breathtaking her costumes were and—most of all—how much she loved working with Boris Karloff. Ms. Marsh also mentioned the original title, *The Black Room Mystery*, and

Gregor ... with his growling voice echoing through nearly-clenched teeth ...

endearingly related to me that she had "quite a good part" in it! I asked her if she would mind signing some stills for me if I sent them with a postpaid return mailer. It would be her pleasure, she assured me. Reluctantly, because I could have listened to her all night, I let her go. With great anticipation, I prepared the package and the postal clerk helped me with getting everything weighed and—I thought—everything was perfect. Warnings are given for good reasons. Six months passed and I reluctantly realized that the stills were not coming back. The conversation, at least, was mine forever.

Over the last 10 years or so, *The Black Room* is finally getting the recognition and appreciation it has always deserved. Hard to understand why it took so long when it is top of the line Karloff in his only triple role (Gregor, Anton, and Gregor as Anton) and has a superb supporting cast, more atmospherics than practically any other Boris Karloff movie, an exquisite song "*Love is Like Music*" and Von the dog. And not least, Roy William Neill directing—the man who made poetry out of *Frankenstein Meets the Wolf Man* and the Rathbone/Bruce Sherlock Holmes series.

Scott Ashlin writing about *The Black Room* in his online column, "1000 Misspent Hours and Counting," says, "The twins grow up to be Boris Karloff; no, this can't possibly end well." Right. The movie starts with the Tyrolean village celebrating the new addition to the baronial de Berghman household. But the heir has a twin, and the family began with the younger twin Brand murdering his older brother, Wolfram, in the black room. "*Principio Et Finem Similia.*" I end as

I began. The Baron believes in the curse and to compound the agony, the doctor (a perfect Edward van Sloan) tells him that the younger brother also has a paralyzed right arm.

The murder room is sealed up. Problem solved. Not so fast. Remember "... this can't possibly end well." Gregor, a completely depraved, unkempt and uncouth fiend is the Baron after the passing of his father. Karloff gives a multi-faceted portrait of this sadist. With his growling voice echoing through nearly-clenched teeth, lounging anything but noble postures, messy hair and cruel expressive eyes, his Gregor is completely comfortable making everyone else uncomfortable. Kindly younger brother Anton returns to the village with the magnificent Thor and appears at the local inn, instantly stopping conversations and the glockenspiel simultaneously because he is the image of the loathed, murdering Baron. Later at the castle, Gregor charms the sweet, unaware Anton into believing that everybody is lying about him. Turns out they're not. Much like Baron Sardonicus, women go to the castle and are as we are told, "... never seen again." After a failed assassination attempt on Gregor at the castle, the brothers de Berghman have dinner at the home of Colonel Hassel (Thurston Hall) and his stunning niece, Thea (Marian Marsh), who entertains them with "*Love is Like Music*," while accompanying herself on the harp. Anton naturally keeps a gracious distance and is a perfect gentleman, while Gregor practically sits on top of the poor girl, leers at her and rudely applauds when she finishes. Also present is Thea's secret love, Lieutenant Lussan

Anton sits and reflects at the large window.

Gregor leers over Thea (Marian Marsh), while she sings and accompanies herself on the harp.

(a stiff but still effective Robert Allen) and lovesick servant–current Gregor girlfriend Mashka (a touching and tragic Katherine de Mille, who was Cecil B. de Mille's adopted daughter and Mrs. Anthony Quinn for 28 years). We see her again later that night as her former sweetheart, Beran (an excellent John Buckler), tries to stop her rendezvous with the Baron. Mashka is in love and determined so now we hear her contralto rendition of "*Love is Like Music*," as Gregor slops over an armchair while eating a pear with a knife. "A pear's the best fruit ... and when you're through with it …" Clearly thinking of Mashka and all the others perhaps, he then hurls what's left of the pear across the room. In a not at all clever move, the jealous-of-Thea-as-possible-Baroness Mashka reveals that she's aware of her fiendish lover moving "heavy things" into the black room at night. Already armed with the pear knife, Gregor uses it on the poor girl which Roy William Neill shows to chilling effect as we see the mirror image of the murderer backing away.

Mashka's disappearance is all the villagers need to storm the castle once more. Beran leads the way and shows his dead sweetheart's shawl (which he obtained from the terrified servant, Peter, played by a terrific Torben Meyer) as damning evidence which convinces Gregor to blurt

out that he is giving up the title to Anton, who finds it "ridiculous." Colonel Hassel and the villagers love the idea, while Anton remains skeptical and—rightly—concerned. Later, not fooling us and not convincing his brother, Gregor merrily talks of being free of his title and lures the

unsuspecting (and as we know doomed) Anton through the fireplace entrance to the black room, where the gentle younger brother sees torture devices and—as the older brother gleefully points out—a pit. Not just any pit, this one gruesomely contains his murdered victims including Mashka, all of whom Anton sees as he leans over putting himself in a perfect position to be kicked down into it by his brother. Before he dies from the fall, we see that he has a bloody knife pressed beside his arm, and facing upwards, he tells Gregor the curse/prophecy "... will be fulfilled ... even from the dead."

Time for Karloff number three which begins straightaway post fratricide. Gregor/Anton looks at himself in the black room wall, (conveniently reflective onyx once the grime is cleared away) smooths back his unruly mop and sneers, "... my dear Thea" (Recall "... This can't possibly end well.") It's a dark pleasure to see the horrific Hyde/Gregor breaking through while he tries to do Jekyll/Anton. Boris Karloff delivers the last part of the de Berghman trio with uncanny skill.

Next up, Colonel Hassel and Gregor/Anton play chess. Apparently, Gregor's masterful game was the only thing that the Colonel liked about him. As expected, marriage with Thea is discussed without her being in the room, and the Colonel is so delighted at the prospective match that he turns over control of all his property to the imposter. Not being a natural lefty, Gregor hesitates over the document and punts, suggesting that they mark the mo-

Gregor continues to rudely stare at Thea in a publicity photo not in the film.

ment with a toast of Thea's favorite cordial. Quickly signing with his never-paralyzed right hand, Gregor is spotted by the Colonel in yet another Roy William Neill brilliant mirror use. Colonel Hassel tricks him into making an ingenious chess move and the game is over in more ways than one. Since Gregor always seems to have a knife handy, he murders the Colonel knowing full well that the uber-jealous-of-Thea Lieutenant Lussan can be easily scapegoated for the crime. The joke of a trial bears that out and the innocent is stripped of his bars and condemned to death. Marian Marsh's Thea is heartbreaking here while Gregor/Anton tells the prosecutor that he doesn't want to testify for fear it will hurt the young man. Of course, he keeps up the game after the Lieutenant is jailed, convincing Thea and Lussan that neither of them wants to see the other.

On the wedding day, Gregor/Anton can barely keep his Hyde side concealed. Karloff has his eyes, his mouth and even his voice constantly giving him away, but the obsequious tailors and delighted villagers don't catch on. He can't resist opening-up the black room pit and gloating over poor lifeless Anton. Gregor is surprised by Thor following him (who knows his beloved master went into the black room and never came out), so the pit stays open. Passionate animal lover Boris must kick at and whip Thor in this scene, which he accomplishes by evil facial expressions and (to our relief and probably his) never touching the dog at

The impressive Von the dog with de Mille, Marsh and Karloff.

all. He nastily snaps at the servants to "get rid" of Thor but our hero (Von as Thor) breaks free of them and is off to the wedding. In the meantime, Mashka's former boyfriend Beran has helped Lussan escape, who then watches the ceremony from a dark recess in the church. Thor enters right on cue at the "speak now or forever hold your peace" moment and lunges at Gregor, who uses his right arm to defend himself. Lussan cries out, "It's the man who murdered Colonel Hassel." Thor leads Lussan and the crowd in chasing Gregor, who is madly whipping the coach horses to get away. (We don't see Karloff hit them, nor do we see him driving the coach in the long shots. It's rear projection in the closeups but well done and minimal). Gregor dashes to the black room. Lussan and the crowd help Thor get in through the fireplace and push the man who murdered his master down into the pit where he is impaled on the knife rigidly still held upright by Anton. Lussan gets the last word, "The prophecy has been fulfilled."

Gregor shares the top spot on a short list of 1930s Karloff evil characters with *The Black Cat's* Hjalmar Poelzig (Universal 1934). Discounting Gregor's chess expertise and Poelzig's architectural abilities, neither one has any humanity, sense of guilt or second thoughts unless it involves their own interests and self-preservation. (Poelzig and de Berghman are both skilled at chess.) Hjalmar tells Vitus that his wife is dead from pneumonia after showing him her body suspended in a glass sarcophagus and that his child died as well. We've already seen his grown-up daughter in the bedroom with Hjalmar, so we know that is not true. Werdegast, doesn't buy the pneumonia story, either. "Lies. All lies, Hjalmar. You killed her. You killed her as I'm about to kill you!" He only finds out later from Joan Alison that his daughter Karen is Madame Poelzig.

A sinister Boris Karloff terrorizes Mashka (Katherine de Mille).

Is the good Anton or the bad Gregor sipping tea?

Gregor, of course, wants no interference in his psychotic, murderous pastimes or possession of the title and will do whatever it takes to keep them going. Hjalmar is a silkier liar than Gregor; he manages to briefly charm the Alisons. Gregor has a harder time keeping his bestial nature concealed. Colonel Hassel and Thea are fooled for a while but, significantly, never Thor. Gregor as Anton breaks through several times with thinly veiled contemptuous behavior in the wedding dressing scene, and his struggle to stop snarling at the villagers thronged near the church as they wish him well.

Before either film Karloff appeared as the title character in *The Mask of Fu Manchu* (MGM 1932). Fu Manchu was no gentlemanly Mr. Wong or even gallows humorous General Wu Yen Fang from *West of Shanghai* (Warner Bros. First National Pictures 1937), "I'm sorry, my friend, in one hour you die ... but I not let you die alone. I come watch." Fu Manchu had one goal: "The British Government—I'll wipe them and the whole accursed white race off the face of the Earth ..." A year later, as the viciously anti-Semitic fictional Prussian Count Ledrantz in *The House of Rothschild* (United Artists 1934), Karloff embodies, "one of

the most detestable non-horror characters of his career ..." according to Scott Allen Nollen, in *Boris Karloff: A Critical Account*

of His Screen, Stage, Radio, Television, and Recording Work. "You won your fight with me, Jew, but remember, victory may have been won too dearly."

After *The Black Room*, the Karloff characters have reasons for their criminality and murders, at least in their own minds. Edmond Bateman in *The Raven* (Universal 1935): "Maybe if a man looks ugly, it makes them do ugly things." However, he does save heroine and hero Jean and Jerry from being crushed in "the room where the walls come together" at the cost of his own life, even with half his face paralyzed courtesy of Lugosi's mad Dr. Vollin. In *The Invisible Ray* (Universal 1936) Karloff's Dr. Janos Rukh eventually poisons himself with his spectacular African find—Radium X—and becomes obsessed with losing both his discovery (to Lugosi's Dr. Felix Benet) and his wife (to a fellow member of the same expedition). While he does manage to kill three expedition members, including Lugosi's Benet, he cannot bring himself to murder his wife because he still loves her. Love and insanity as rationalizations for bad behavior happen here not for the first time or the last. After all, Boris' Imhotep/Ardath Bey's character in *The Mummy* (Universal 1932) had to been insane after being horrifically buried alive for thousands of years. But still he loves and tells Princess Anck-es-en-amon, reincarnated as Helen Grosvenor, that she cannot join him "...

He is dressed as Anton, but look at the cruel mouth and you know it is Gregor.

Colonel Hassel (Thurson Hall) thinks he is turning over his land to the good Anton.

fight so that he can kill in "hot blood." Awful and dangerous as he is, Mord does have one moment of hesitation when he's sent to the Tower to dispatch Edward V and his brother Richard Duke of York, who preceded Richard in the line of succession. He sends two assistants in to murder them because he cannot face destroying the innocent little boys himself.

If we believe that Hjalmar Poelzig did love Werdegast's wife, and accept as fact his self-pitying, "Are we any the less victims of the war than those whose bodies were torn asunder? Are we not both the living dead?" which is a stretch. Then we must award *The Black Room's* Baron Gregor de Berghman the crown for the most evil and remorseless 1930's Karloff character.

At a tight 67 minutes we are never bored with *The Black Room*. Karloff is the center but never overplays, which results in a star vehicle with an ensemble vibe. The love scenes are engaging and brief. The dialogue never lags and sparkles with snaps of biting humor. All the under-fives [characters with five lines or less] and background actors are good. Roy William Neill gives us a moody Grimm's fairy-tale horror movie which ends well, but not cutely.

CREDITS: Director: Roy William Neill; Producer: Robert North; Screenplay: Henry Myers and Arthur Strawn, Based on a story by Arthur Strawn; Cinematographer: Allen G. Siegler; Editor: Richard Cahoon; Art Director: Stephen Goosson; Musical Director: Louis Silvers; Costume Director: Murray Mayer

CAST: Boris Karloff (Baron Gregor de Berghman/Anton de Berghman); Marian Marsh (Thea Hassel); Robert Allen (Lieutenant Albert Lussan); Thurston Hall (Colonel Hassel); Katherine De Mille (Mashka); John Buckler (Beran); Torben Meyer (Peter); Egon Brecher (Karl); John M. Bleifer (Franz); Fredrik Vogeding (Josef); Lois Lindsey, Phyllis Fraser (Bridesmaids); John Maurice Sullivan (Archbishop); Reginald Pasch (Tailor); Robert Middlemass (Prosecuting Attorney); Marian Lessing (Marie); Henry Kolker (Baron Frederick de Berghman); Edward Van Sloan (Doctor); The Bleifer twins (Anton and Gregor as boys); Von the Dog (Thor)

until you are ready to face moments of horror for an eternity of love."

His John Ellman in *The Walking Dead* (Warner Bros. First National 1936)—one of the most heartrending of Karloff portrayals—never actually kills the people who framed him for a judge's murder, but after being unjustly executed, acts as an instrument of divine retribution before dying for the second time. The same year in *The Man Who Changed His Mind* (Gaumont-British Pictures 1936), the actor's Dr. Laurience repeats the same love and insanity motif. Unrequited love for his assistant, Claire, and crazy, determined efforts to switch minds between people. While still in England, he played the not so innocent Dr. Victor Sartorius in *Juggernaut* (Grand National Pictures 1936), who cannot claim love or insanity as an excuse for accepting a hit job on an elderly patient in return for funding his research for "a cure for certain types of ataxic paralysis." In fact, Sartorius starts the Karloff slew of doctors, medical researchers and scientists who justify murder as a necessary means to a laudable end. Saying, "I'm in the middle of a most interesting experiment …"and needing £20,000 to finish it doesn't absolve his guilt.

After a string of more-or-less innocent victims—Gravelle, *Charlie Chan at the Opera*

(20th Century Fox 1937); Dave Mallory, *Night Key* (Universal 1937); Jevries, *The Invisible Menace* (Warner Bros. 1938) and the Monster, *Son of Frankenstein* (Universal 1939)—there's Dr. Henryk Savaard in *The Man They Could Not Hang* (Columbia 1939) and Mord in *Tower of London* (Universal 1939). Dr. Savaard continues the string of questionable doctors started with Dr. Sartorius. Although his motives are purer, foreshadowing organ and heart transplants and pre-surgical procedures, he is bitter after his resuscitation, only wanting vengeance on those responsible for his execution. He even murders Lang his faithful assistant, who brought him back to life but surrenders to save his daughter Janet's life with his own mechanical heart, which he destroys before he dies. Dr. Savaard partially redeems himself, which Dr. Sartorius never does. The 1930s finished up with Karloff's sadistic Mord in *Tower of London*. Karloff's fictional executioner character seems to enjoy torture and begs his master, Richard III, to allow him to

Ealing Studios present another comedy:

ALEC GUINNESS
JOAN GREENWOOD
CECIL PARKER in

THE SCIENCE IN FANTASY BY DON MANKOWSKI

THE MAN IN
THE WHITE SUIT

A MICHAEL BALCON PRODUCTION   DIRECTED BY ALEXANDER MACKENDRICK

Super Cloth

In a factory, an automated loom spins a bolt of beautiful white material as men in neat, drab business suits look on with suspicious interest. A laborer removes the finished product, then tries to tear off the last trailing thread, something she's clearly done thousands of times. But the thread injures her finger. One man must step forward with a fine blowtorch to cut the thread with an intense flame.

What's going on here?

It's just one odd moment in a very odd science fiction film of 1951, a clever satire of British industry, *The Man in the White Suit.*

"Now that calm and sanity have returned to the textile industry," says a solemn narrator as the film begins, "I feel it my duty to reveal something of the true story behind the recent crisis. A story, which we were—happily—able to keep out of the newspapers at the time …" The scene fades to the beginnings of the recent unpleasantness to which the man refers.

We are in the Northern part of Great Britain at the midpoint of the previous century. The setting is a pair of textile

factories that deal in artificial fibers. Michael Corland (Michael Gough) is happy to show his competitor Alan Birnley (Cecil Parker) around his site. Corland hopes

Sidney Stratton (Alec Guinness), in a publicly photo, defends himself in his white suit.

to borrow funds from Birnley, and also marry the man's daughter, Daphne (Joan Greenwood [wife of André Morell]). Birnley turns out to be our narrator.

White Collars and the Blues

So, these competing mills are in fact huge kingdoms about to be united by marriage—probably to the detriment of the serf-like workers. Among the laborers is Sidney Stratton (Alec Guinness), whom we will learn is a brilliant student, acting as a lowly glass washer in order to conduct unapproved experiments. Sidney is motivated by a vision, a technological one.

Corland cannot explain one peculiar experimental apparatus that Birnley stumbles upon. The tableau involves a huge distillation tube, tall refluxing columns, stout flasks, much tubing and whatnot. It sputters and grinds merrily away, producing *something* with slow determination, as the businessmen puzzle over it. The renegade experiment is traced to Sidney.

"No, Mister Corland, you're not firing me: I've resigned … I did what I did because there was no other way." It's an impressive speech that Sidney delivers about his qualifications (he once had a fellowship at Cambridge), the importance of his work and the short-sightedness of the managers and of the success that he'll one day enjoy—but it's only to a lavatory mirror. The actual defense must have been less effective, for Sidney has been fired.

At once he looks for work at another textile mill. It must be a mill, he tells the man at the employment exchange who knows him quite well: this has happened seven times already. Naturally, Sidney ends up at Birnley's mill. It is here that he meets Bertha (Vida Hope), a working class girl who is highly suspicious of "capital," and involved in fighting for the rights of the laborers.

Sidney drools at the laboratories. He is charged with hauling a newfangled electron microscope up to one of them, and causally tells a couple of company scientists how to best use the instrument. His expertise earns him a small corner of a lab bench with which to continue his experiment.

The Stratton incident has had a negative effect upon Corland's plans for expansion, what with the loss of Birnley's approval. Daphne, the daughter and prospective bride, is of course dismayed as well. When the young woman discovers the troublesome Sidney in her father's plant, she is about to expose him. He begs for just a moment to explain what he's trying to do. Daphne is at first bewildered by his explanation, but is a fast learner. She does know what an atom is, and that's a start. Molecules, he explains, are atoms stuck together in this case like a long chain.

Factory workers look over the mysterious lab to learn about the new discovery.

Making it Perfectly Clear

"Now, cotton and silk and every natural fiber is made up of these chains," explains Sidney. "And, recently, we've learned to make artificial fibers with even longer chains, such as rayon and nylon—you've heard of nylon? Well, I think I've succeeded in the copolymerization of amino acid residues and carbohydrate molecules, both containing ionic groups. It's really simple. I believe I've got the right catalyst to promote interaction between the reactive groups at the end of the peptide chains and the carbohydrate combination, while the charges of the ionic groups will cross link the chains and confer valuable elastic properties. Why at high temperature and pressure ..."

Heavy hydrogen and radioactive elements are also involved, it would appear. Daphne's slowly expanding smile shows that she is won over by the man's enthusiasm. Sidney is able to continue his clandestine work in the off hours, making use of the electron microscope to check his results. Bertha is annoyed that Sidney is laboring for nothing, undermining her labor efforts.

Sidney's eccentricities have the other chemists up in arms, and they're ready to get rid of him. "You can't fire me," he exclaims, correctly. "I don't work here!" Some steps in his synthesis are so explosion-prone that he has to trigger them from a distance. But, when things go right, the clear liquid bubbling in his flasks turns a luminous shade of white.

In order to get Birnley's attention, Sidney has to invade the man's house. Again, a sacking seems imminent, but this time Daphne intervenes. She astonishes her father by explaining the uses of a molecule of "infinite length, with optimum inter-chain attractions." She's been studying chemistry. Why, she explains, to break such a fiber you'd have to split the molecule. Moreover, a surface charge of static electricity would repel dirt and grime. (I hope that she meant "indefinite length" or "indeterminate length." A molecule of infinite length would literally take forever to synthesize.)

Hot Stuff

Sidney gets to go on experimenting, with a blank check from Birnley. "Radioactive thorium? What's he want that for?" As if in response, a loud *boom* is heard as

Alec Guinness and Joan Greenwood (Daphne) lock eyes in the street.

Howard Marion-Crawford, Ernest Thesiger and Desmond Roberts' characters believe Sidney's invention will hurt the textile industry.

the building shakes. There are *many* explosions. The press are getting curious, but are successfully misled. (I certainly hope that *nuclear* explosions aren't taking place. The radioactive elements are more likely atomic tracers to explore the synthesis.)

Birnley and Corland defy orders and are standing by Sidney's lab bench at a critical moment. Indeed, Sidney initiates the final step by remote control from a well-padded bunker. There's no explosion, but instead the glowing white substance is formed.

Things are moving fast now. The liquid produces a fiber, machine tested for strength. It breaks the machine! Now, the fiber is spun into brilliant white cloth. When the loom-tender makes to snap off the trailing thread with a practiced gesture, she cuts her finger on it. Sidney produces a cutting torch. "Fortunately, there's a chemical change at three hundred degrees centigrade." The cloth is tested. Dark ink is poured onto it, but it beads up and rolls off, leaving the cloth as white as ever.

As Sidney is measured for the prototype suit, he explains that the material can be sewn, as needles will simply pass between the threads, but that the components will have to be cut from patterns with the high-temperature torch. The cloth is necessarily white, as it resists dye as much as dirt. By varying the intermediates, he will be able to produce synthetic wool, cotton, linen and whatever. This talk perplexes the tailor (Miles Malleson) to no end.

Soon, Sidney is able to model the miracle suit for Daphne. "It makes you look like a knight in shining armor. That's what you are," she tells him. "Don't you understand what this means? Millions of people all over the world, living lives of drudgery, fighting an endless, losing battle against shabbiness and dirt. You've won that battle for them. You've set them free. The whole world's going to bless you."

That's *one* view. Mr. Birnley wants to announce the breakthrough. It's Corland who is concerned. He makes an urgent telephone call to Sir John Kierlaw, evidently a legend in the textile business, now enjoying retirement. The mysterious Sir John (Ernest Thesiger) orders a meeting and hurries to attend. As Birnley argues for continuing in the name of progress, Kierlaw agrees with Corland that the breakthrough threatens the industry.

The laborers at once mirror the divide of the businessmen. Bertha beholds Sidney in his wonder suit and is optimistic—until the other workers bring her back to earth. "It

never wears out? We'll have just one lot to make, and that's the end of it. Everyone will be laid off." Clearly, Sidney is dangerous.

The late 1940s and early 1950s were exciting times for synthetic fibers. But, just what is a synthetic fiber? Could such a magical thread exist?

Carbon

Let's start at the beginning: Carbon. Carbon is the most versatile of the elements. Look at graphite: slippery, but useful on stubborn gears and locks. Or coal: lumpy and dirty but welcome in the winter, glowing in a fire. Then there are diamonds: transparent, brilliant and precious. But *they're all just carbon*. It's simply striking a different pose in each role—only the arrangement of the atoms is different.

Carbon is just reactive enough (at temperatures and pressure familiar to us, which is what matters) that it can be forced, by gentle heating or chemical catalysts, into useful combinations with other elements. At the same time, it is just sluggish enough that such compounds tend to stay put when left alone afterward. No small advantages these. Compared to carbon, most of the other elements combine rarely or slowly or refuse to combine at all; or else they combine *too* readily, in conflagrations or explosions.

Each carbon atom is capable of forming four chemical bonds in three dimensions with other atoms. Moreover, carbon favors "covalent" bonds based upon the sharing of electrons. These bonds have a plasticity not found in metallic or ionic bonds that the other elements are prone to form. Or rather, these bonds are what *convey* plasticity upon plastics.

More interestingly, carbon can utilize double and triple bonds within its quota of four, and has no objections to bonding with other carbon atoms, in long chains and joints and rings if given the opportunity. Most of the other elements have

"The whole world is going to bless you." Sidney's eyes say not so fast.

too few bonds available to be useful, or too many to be workable, or else these just refuse to form chains of any appreciable length.

Indeed, carbon's versatility is such that there are many *more* possible carbon compounds than non-carbon compounds, even given that carbon is but one of over a hundred known elements. Organic chemistry is the branch of the science devoted primarily to carbon compounds. The organic chemist has a far richer toolbox than the inorganic chemist.

These noteworthy features are, almost certainly, why the phenomenon known as "life" depends upon carbon in order to happen. Nothing else with those qualities exists in sufficient quantity on earth to permit the diversity required in the numbers required. (Silicon is the element most similar to carbon, but it's a poor substitute, tending towards less useful bonds, and it doesn't form long chains. Furthermore, it's scarcer than carbon, and what silicon there is on earth is usually bound up in rocks.)

Consider the organic world at its most basic. *Methane* is just one carbon atom with the minimum adornment: it's linked to four hydrogen atoms. It's a colorless, odorless gas. (That's right: odorless. Swamp gas gets its infamous aroma from other stuff like hydrogen sulfide.) Stick two methane molecules together (to do that, you just lose a couple hydrogens and link their orphaned chemical bonds) and you have *ethane*, which is only slightly more complex.

Joan Greenwood and Michael Gough

Sir John and Michael Corland lead the charge on poor Sidney.

The Amazing Double Bond

Ethylene is ethane with double-bonded carbon atoms and fewer hydrogen, and *acetylene* is the triply bonded version. These are simple hydrocarbons. The chemical bonds in hydrocarbons represent a store of energy that can be released by combining them with oxygen, i.e., by burning them. The double and triple bonds are particularly energy-rich.

You can picture methane as a tetrahedron—that is, a solid with four triangular sides—with a carbon atom hidden in the center and a hydrogen atom at each vertex. Ethane would look like two of these methane tetrahedra touching at one point, one *vertex* of each. Ethylene would look like two methane tetrahedra joined along a line, an *edge* common to both. Acetylene would look like two tetrahedra with one entire triangular *side* in common.

Acetylene is very reactive. Its intensely hot flame is used in cutting torches. However, if instead of just burning it to enjoy the heat you let it react with hydrochloric acid, you get something called chloroethene, or vinyl chloride. It's still pretty simple, but the simple molecule contains the reactive double bond and a chlorine atom.

When striving for durable end products, the goal is something that will be especially *non*-reactive once the special conditions are removed. Perhaps para-

doxically, the most reactive elements are important for stability. When liberated in the lab, these elements attack other atoms and molecules violently. But, once stuck in place, they're almost impossible to pull loose. They're rather like congressmen.

Fluorine is the most reactive of the elements. Despite intensive efforts, no chemist had even been able to study fluorine in its pure state until 1886, when it was finally pried free of its compounds and safely isolated. It was discovered that fluorine gas would attack other compounds readily, and once a compound was fluorinated, dammit, it was fluorinated for good. Teflon is a polymer that's saturated with fluorine atoms, so it takes a lot of effort to stain or scratch Teflon.

Enter Chlorine

Chlorine, part of the fluorine family, is somewhat less reactive, but still useful. It's also easier to obtain, and that's important. Chlorine was isolated in quantity for gas weaponry in World War I, so contemptible a tactic that civilized nations have disavowed its use ever since. But chlorine has its peaceful uses.

Simple chlorinated hydrocarbons are inherently useful as cleaning agents (such as chloroform and carbon tetrachloride), and insect controls (like dichlorodiphenyltrichloroethane, DDT). But there's more that you can do with them.

Those occasional atomic interlopers, such as chlorine in hydrocarbons,

Sidney is being descended upon by the higher-ups of the factory.

are useful. Organic chemists discovered processes involving these chlorinated hydrocarbons that could be used to link the small carbon chains into big ones. Now, if you put a bunch of paper clips in a bag, you wouldn't expect them to form a long chain, not even if you shook the silly bag for many hours.

But you *can* do it with a "bag" of small molecules with carbon atoms, after a fashion. It isn't magic: The chemist merely creates conditions that favor one sort of chemical combination over another, and the atoms do what comes naturally. They break off their ancestral compound and fly off to unions that are currently more attractive, leaving behind broken chemical bonds. The orphaned electrons in the abandoned bonds are compelled to seek out new connections. (Isn't personification *fun*?)

The manner in which the small two or three-carbon units are linked can be controlled by varying the conditions of the reaction. One can vary the temperature. The pressure. The acidity, alkalinity or neutrality of the environment. The presence or absence of oxygen, nitrogen, chlorine and other gases. The presence of metallic catalysts. Any and all of these can affect the properties of the resulting compound.

Will a process form long, straight chains, or complicated branched ones? Will the side-chains be long and straight or bulky and bunched? Will it form the occasional double or triple bond, and how often? What sorts of impurities should be introduced, and what level tolerated—or required?

That's the science of organic chemistry: determining what will result from all of this. Much of the success was achieved via trial and error, guesses and messes.

Thousands and Thousands

Polyvinyl chloride (PVC) results from linking thousands and thousands of vinyl chloride units. Getting back to our models, PVC would look like thousands of those little tetrahedral pyramids linked up, touching at the vertices, or occasionally the edges, with chlorine atoms spaced out on alternate links, stretching out as far as the eye can see (on this particular scale). PVC is slightly flexible and very tough, and can be used for plumbing.

Now, ethylene terephthalate (ET) is an "ester," has a molecule somewhat more complicated than vinyl chloride—it involves 10 carbon atoms, six of them in a ring, and four oxygen atoms—but it can be polymerized into poly-ET, the most important of the group known as polyesters, which are useful in many applications, including clothing.

Natural cloth is spun from plant fibers or animal hair. These consist of short protein molecules with a few carbon atoms in a simple chain, plus hydrogen, some oxygen and nitrogen atoms and miscellaneous. Spun together, these have some semblance of a continuous thread. Woven together in a pattern, they have some semblance of a continuous sheet. But, you can tear ordinary cloth rather easily, because you're simply pulling relatively short, nested threads out of their ordered alignment by overcoming friction.

Synthetic cloth, with carbon chains thousands of atoms long can be made much tougher. (Co-polymerization, mentioned by Stratton, involves two different monomers, i.e., building blocks. We'll be getting back to Stratton.)

Molecules used to be demonstrated to students via ball and stick, tinker-toy models, with electrons presumably in orbit about the atomic nuclei. The modern theory has a molecule's electrons surrounding the backbone of the nuclei in a "probability" cloud. Perceived in this manner, a long chain molecule looks formidable. It takes a lot of energy to break those chemical bonds once they've stabilized.

The Chains that Bind

So, that's what Sidney Stratton has produced, a long, seamless polymer that resists breaking or cutting. (There's some blather about branched chains. Actually, molecules with unbranched chains are generally denser and tougher, but this *sounds* better). Of course the remarkable thread can be woven into remarkable cloth, a fabric than cannot be worn out or torn easily.

Not only does Stratton Cloth refuse to be stained, it actually repels dirt and grime, probably via some sort of electronic-magnetic field that it generates. Stratton's amazing thread won't hold dye or color—it repels these as well. This apparent drawback makes the discovery seem all the more real, and gives the film its name. Clothes made from it will be the purest white. Sidney speculates that it

Sidney and Michael Corland

may be possible to introduce color at an earlier stage, but for the time being, the future looks snowy.

No more dirty or worn clothes! A boon to mankind, eh? This theory is discarded rapidly. The invention unites the people—against it.

Sidney's pseudochemical babble sounds realistic enough. The references to radioactive elements and heavy hydrogen play upon hot topics in the scientific world of the time. Just perhaps, the talk of amino acid residues and peptide chains suggests that there may be some *biological* basis for the suit's robustness. It would be paradoxical indeed to give life to a garment so that it could no longer be killed. But it would not necessarily be magic. Scientists have considered cultivating mutant bacteria to take part in microtechnology. Perhaps Stratton's method involves some sort of protoliving microbe spinning out an incredibly thin metallic backbone for the miracle fiber. (Were I scripting a remake, I'd definitely employ this approach in my pseudoscientific babble.)

Of course, here's where the old suspension of disbelief becomes necessary.

Sidney (Alec Guinness) with factory workers Vida Hope and Duncan Lamont

The Downsides of Paradise

I'm pretty sure that someone could make a suit nearly impervious to harm, even in 1951. (Hell, weren't they doing this with chain mail in the days of King Arthur?) But I'm also sure that it wouldn't be comfortable: probably too heavy, too hot, too hideous … or all three. I'm sure there'd be a trade-off.

What of *esthetic* concerns? Remember those polyester suits that were very popular in the 1970s? They wouldn't wrinkle, washed easily, dried swiftly and didn't need pressing.

How often do you see that material now? Nobody wants to wear that stuff. People noticed that those clothes looked awful. Natural fibers, due to their imperfections, have diversity; something called "texture." Synthetic fibers are boring in their sameness, in their blasted perfection. A woolen jacket looks and feels soft and warm. Polyester pants look and feel harsh.

Remember, until Stratton figures out an answer to the dye problem, it's going to be a white-suited world, or so it would appear. Will the toughest material always be the most desired? Of course not. If that were true, army duds would have been in fashion throughout history.

What of the *stylistic* concern? So, people will never stop wearing anything so long as it's wearable? A Stratton Suit looks so good that no one will ever want to wear anything else?

I think that Volkswagen tried that with automobiles. Some people appreciated the fact that their parts remained interchangeable year after year. Others wanted something different, even if it cost a bit more. The latter group considerably outnumbers the former.

So nobody's going to want to ditch the three-button model for a two-button version? Nobody's going to want side vents or notched lapels or four buttons on the sleeve or a ticket pocket or something else? Where does all that stuff at the Salvation Army come from? Some people must have gotten tired of it even while it was still wearable

Might not the everlasting suit become a staple of the lower classes, while those who can afford it go back to more natural cuts of cloth in the most fashionable new shapes? Even if your clothes lasted as long as your automobile, you're going to change them sometime.

What of the *biological* concern? Won't kids need bigger and bigger clothes as they grow? Will everybody wear hand-me-downs? So you've put on a few pounds, or slimmed down. Won't you need new clothing that fits? Won't rebellious kids want to vary from the standard? Who really wants to inherit the family suit from several generations back?

What of the *hygienic* concern? If the outside of your clothes repels sweat and stain, then so would the inside. It's not pleasant to contemplate, but on a warm day, you could get awfully slippery within your pristine duds. Instead of suggesting cleanliness, the sight of a white suit might be a stimulus to hold one's nose.

What of the *safety* concern: What happens if you're severely injured while wearing a Stratton Suit? The suit may protect the wearer from some scrapes and cuts, but unfortunately wouldn't prevent him from being battered or squashed. Wouldn't emergency surgery have to wait while your doctor calls in a cutting torch-skilled paramedic specialist to carefully cut you out of your clothes? A really old joke is reborn: "He's gonna *die*, but don't his suit look nice?"

Don't laugh; there'd be a whole new class of injuries. Think of all the times you snagged your cuff or sleeve or got your necktie or scarf caught somewhere. Now, imagine the same thing, only you *don't* tear free: you're pinned somewhere at best, perhaps dragged half a block, strangled at worst. People who work with certain types of machinery have to avoid rings, bracelets and necklaces. Stratton Clothing would be a similar risk. We saw in the film how the seamstress injured her finger trying to snap off the remainder of the thread—that's only the beginning.

What of the *legislative* concern? I can see more government intervention required. Of course, Stratton Cloth might require distinctive markings. If you fool-

Sidney seems to be hiding behind an intricate machine.

ishly used some of it to wipe window glass, never mind costly lenses, it might ruin the surface. Imagine what would happen when Stratton Thread is mistaken for dental floss.

What of the *environmental* concern? Think of the problems of *disposing of* Stratton Clothes when they're truly no longer needed. It would be a problem similar to that with used tires and motor oil these days. (Yes, I know they're never supposed to be discarded, but we've already raised some doubt as to that bit of wisdom.) The law might require that the cloth be unraveled and the fibers re-used. (This would create more jobs, but unappealing ones.)

What of the *legal* concern? I wonder if a criminal outfitted in a Stratton Jumpsuit could squirm through barbed wire and crash through glass without much effort and harm, rendering rudimentary security systems ineffective. The police might have to ban the stuff in some areas.

Labor

Oh yes, what of the *labor* concern? Well, what of it? Here's an area with which the film does concern itself, but perhaps it's a misguided concern.

So there's less need for washing and sewing. Who's to say that new jobs wouldn't create themselves, perhaps in unanticipated ways? The film indicates that it requires a high-temperature torch to cut out the suit patterns from the Stratton Cloth. The new world might require fewer tailors, but those that found work in the trade would be skilled profession-

als working with dangerous equipment, and these would be able to demand just compensation after enough amateurs immolated themselves.

When people of my grandparents' generation bought one of the early television sets, they practically required a live-in repairman who was always replacing tubes. Transistors changed all that. I've had TV sets that performed admirably without attention for 10 years. Did this kill the industry? Or did we all buy more electronic devices and support more innovation and more jobs? I rest my case.

You're not *supposed* to ask such questions, certainly not after half a century. The fantasy element is that the miracle material looks great, feels great and has that permanency. Even in good science fiction, it's okay to break a rule of the universe now and again, so long as you play fair after doing so and do not heap on

even more improbabilities. This snappy little film does reasonably well at convincing us. It's perfectly obvious that it spells eventual doom for the garment industry.

Cover Up

In the boardroom at Birnley Textiles, there's a tense signing ceremony supervised by Sir John. Sidney learns that he is to be paid for his silence. The discovery is to be suppressed.

Sidney won't hear of it. He tries to escape, makes a go of it, but is knocked out in the foyer when a bust that he jars causes a large painting to drop on his head. I have no clue as to the subjects of the bust and the painting. By rights, the former should have depicted a rich capitalist and the latter a celebration of the worker, as the two groups unite against the threatening discovery. Well, the bust must be a company hero, and the painting does feature some friendly hand holding visible to a brief glimpse.

"Is he all right?" asks Birnley.

"Yes," says the man examining the unconscious inventor.

"Pity," adds Sir John Kierlaw.

Birnley keeps Sidney at the factory under house arrest, until all can figure out what to do. ("We can't keep him here forever," frets Birnley, "I mean there are one or two *laws* in the country …") Rumors of the great discovery have circulated. Despite denials, textile stocks are falling. The workers are talking of a general strike.

Obviously, Stratton isn't tempted by money: they've offered him a quarter million pounds to keep quiet. Perhaps a woman would succeed. Daphne is solicited to provide some sweet talk to Sidney, and reluctantly goes along. But, Sidney resists her charms. "Thank you Sidney," she says, relieved. "If you would've said 'yes' I'd have strangled you!" Daphne resolves to help Sidney escape.

Escape

Sidney climbs out his window and lowers himself to the ground on a thin strand of his own miraculous thread. The very proper film goes a bit slapstick as Sidney flees. Lacking a shilling for a cab, he visits his old flat, to the dismay of the new renter. Bertha sees him as a threat and won't help him. His only ally is a little girl (Mandy Miller). This is noteworthy: only monsters and menaces who are good at heart have the confidence of children

Now, capital and labor are united against Sidney Stratton. The managers join the workers in pursuit. As Sidney tries to hide, his glowing white suit betrays him. He chances upon his former landlady, Mrs. Watson (Edie Martin), and begs her for some darker clothes from the pile she carries. "Why can't you scientists leave things alone?" asks the woman, putting a very human face to it all. "What about my bit of washing when there's no washing to do?"

The matter will be resolved in admirably simple fashion, which I won't reveal here. A subtle audio hint suggests that we may be in for more misadventure.

The Man in the White Suit

The Man in the White Suit is a 1951 release from Ealing Studios, the folks who brought you the classic horror of *Dead of Night* (1945) and the classic comedy of *The Lavender Hill Mob* (also 1951).

A marvelously contrived film, it never seems to be trying very hard to be funny, and is all the more effective for this. It's a rare look at the downside of Utopia, the dark side of a miracle, with echoes of the Midas Touch and the Golden Goose.

The script, by Roger Macdougall, John Dighton and Alexander Mackendrick manages to mention radioactive elements, heavy hydrogen, and amino acids, all hot scientific topics in the 1950s. Though included for comedic effect, it should be noted that explosions are a very real threat for the organic chemist: trinitrotoluene (TNT) is just four short steps removed from the common solvent benzene: just a methyl group and three nitro groups and you're there—and you'd better not stay there too long. Chemists will sympathize with the plight of poor Mr. Harrison, who gets interrupted while sucking on a pipette, and gags a bit each time it happens.

Alec Guinness leads a fine cast of British professionals, going from tweedy nerd to shining knight to the unlikely maniacal threat to life as we know it. He uses facial expressions to great effect but never descends to mugging, and is truly charming in his determination. Cecil Parker is all bluster swiftly turned to bewilderment over it all. His performance was allegedly based on Ealing studio chief Michael Balcon. Pretty Joan Greenwood delivers some profound lines in her husky voice.

In a wonderful supporting role, Ernest Thesiger is evil and greed personified as the elderly and fragile Sir John. Miles Malleson's puzzled tailor is hilarious with minimal effort. Olaf Olsen suggests Peter Lorre as a sycophantic henchman.

In Thesiger, Guinness, and Gough the film manages to unite icons of three popular and influential science fiction franchises, spanning six decades, respectively *[Bride of] Frankenstein*, *Star Wars* and *Batman*.

While the bosses pursue Sidney, elderly Sir John is the last to tumble into a crowded bus. "Room for one more inside" says the driver, paraphrasing the infamous quote from *Dead of Night*.

The music score by Benjamin Frankel is tense and determined, like the film's subject. A real achievement in audio is Stratton's lab apparatus. It comments upon the action by burbling, guzzling, wheezing and tooting, managing to sound contented, disputatious, scolding or merry as the general mood demands. The special effects are rudimentary, but effective enough.

There are no spaceships, aliens, or brain transplants here. Despite its light directorial touch, Alexander McKendrick's film explores the effect of technological advances on the human condition. That, my friends, is what science fiction is supposed to do, and is what this film does so very well.

The Man in the White Suit

Directed by Alexander Mackendrick. Produced by Michael Balcon. Screenplay by Roger Macdougall, John Dighton and Alexander Mackendrick, from a play by Roger Macdougall.

Alec Guinness (Sidney Stratton), Joan Greenwood (Daphne), Cecil Parker (Birnley), Michael Gough (Michael Corland), Ernest Thesiger (Sir John Kierlaw), Howard Marion Crawford (Cranford), Vida Hope (Bertha), Henry Mollison (Hoskins), Miles Malleson (tailor), Patric Doonan (Frank), Duncan Lamont (Harry), Harold Goodwin (Wilkins), Colin Gordon (Hill), Russell Waters (Davidson), Joan Harben (Miss Johnson), Olaf Olsen (Knudsen), Edie Martin (Mrs. Watson), Mandy Miller (Gladdie).

Ealing Studios, 1951. 82m

BY GREG MANK

PUSSYFOOTING
THE CAT CREEPS
UNIVERSAL'S LAST GASP OF HORROR

The celebrated golden age of Universal horror officially began September 29, 1930, when a horse-drawn carriage drove down a hill on Universal's back lot. It was the first day's shooting of *Dracula*.

It unceremoniously ended on January 17, 1946, when a group of players, a black cat, and the black cat's stand-in worked on Stage 15. It was the last day's shooting of *The Cat Creeps*.

Dracula had been a horror epic, starring the legendary Bela Lugosi and power-packed with sex, sacrilege, and blasphemy. *The Cat Creeps* was a double bill "B" quickie, featuring a no-name cast, upstaged by a trained feline who received on-the-set pampering that none of the human actors enjoyed.

It was *Dracula* that had baptized Universal's sound horror era. It was *The Cat Creeps* that bestowed a lethargic Last Rites.

There were, of course, other Universal horror films that followed, but those came from Universal-International, after the studio took on new management. *The Cat Creeps* was the final product made during the officially recognized halcyon era of 1930 to 1946.

Is it better than its lousy reputation suggests? It would have to be. At its best, *The Cat Creeps'* 58 minutes offers vague homages to *The Old Dark House*, *Mark of the Vampire* and, not surprisingly, *Cat People*. It also features an oddly intimate connection to Universal's glory days—namely, 1931's *Frankenstein*.

At any rate, it's possible that this might be the last issue of *Midnight Marquee*. In tribute, I present this retrospect on what was the last of the Universal horror movies.

By 1946, the basic property that became *The Cat Creeps* hadn't tallied nine lives, but it was working on it.

First, there'd been the play *The Cat and the Canary*, by John Willard, and which had opened at Broadway's National Theatre February 7, 1922. Willard appeared in the play as well as having written it, and the cast featured Henry Hull, 13 years away from starring in Universal's *Werewolf of London*.

In 1927, Universal made a silent film of *The Cat and the Canary*, starring Laura La Plante. The director was German

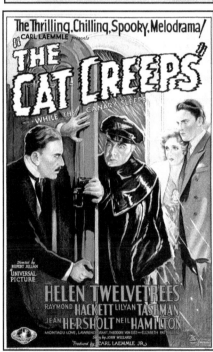

Posters for Universal's 1927 *The Cat and the Canary* and 1930's *The Cat Creeps*.

Expressionist Paul Leni. It was arguably Hollywood's greatest "haunted house" mystery to that time.

In 1930, Universal produced *The Cat Creeps*, starring Helen Twelvetrees. The film, co-directed by Rupert Julian (of 1925's *The Phantom of the Opera*) and John Willard (who'd penned the play), had come from Universal's gates three months before the premiere of *Dracula*. Indeed, if one accepts the 1930 version as the first of Universal's sound era horrors (few do, as it was a mystery thriller, more than a horror show), the cycle both began and ended with a film titled *The Cat Creeps*. Alas, the 1930 version is lost.

On June 14, 1937, *The Cat and the Canary* had a Broadway revival at the Majestic Theatre. It lasted only nine performances.

Universal lost the rights to Paramount, which produced 1939's *The Cat and the Canary*, starring Bob Hope and Paulette Goddard. It was a tip-top horror comedy, directed by Elliot Nugent, and featured in its cast George Zucco and Gale Sondergaard.

Then, come 1945, Universal decided to make a film titled *The Cat Creeps*. The title would possibly remind horror fans—the older ones, at least—of the 1927 and 1930 film versions ... and perhaps the 1939 Paramount hit. The plot would concern a spooky old house, a crooked lawyer, and just enough rip-offs from the original scenario to *seem* a remake of the venerable old chestnut. Universal breezily proceeded with this mutant, unsanctioned version and the surviving budget sheet for *The Cat Creeps* tells the tale—the studio spent absolutely nothing for the story rights.

John Willard was in no position to do anything about it. He'd died in 1942.

A script was completed February 28, 1945, 10 months before shooting started. On March 5, 1945, Joseph Breen of the Production Code wrote to Maurice Pivar, a Universal executive, about several troublesome details. Among them:

Page 10: We think it would be well to finish Bill's speech, "You see I thought you were that—

Lois Collier, leading lady of *The Cat Creeps*, takes a stroll with Smoky the black cat, who was the true star of the show.

Iris Clive, aka Iris Lancaster, as "Kyra Goran," the mysterious "Cat Lady" of *The Cat Creeps*. The actress had been the lover of Colin Clive, who played the title role in Universal's *Frankenstein*, and had died in 1937.

that —" by possibly using the word "boy." This, to avoid possible offense to Negroes who might think any other word was implied at this time ...

Page 39: In O'Toole's first speech, "Eddie, I just gotta go an' —," we request that this be completed inoffensively since as now written it is open to the suggestion of a toilet reference ...

Page 82: Connie's two uses of the word "witch" at the bottom of this page should be pronounced carefully so there can be no possible confusion with the unacceptable word "bitch."

Page 123, scene 272: We assume that care will be exercised where Gay is shown hanging by

the seat of her skirt. And on page 124, scene 276, there must be no unacceptable exposure of her person where she falls from the tree after her dress is torn ...

Sound like a fun movie? Well, over the next nine months, the project, with story by Gerald Geraghty (who primarily scripted Westerns), and script by Edward Dein (who'd contributed on Val Lewton's *The Leopard Man*) and Jerry Warner (who'd worked on the screenplay for Universal's 1946 *Girl on the Spot*), dropped any black character; there was no one named Bill, or Eddie or O'Toole; nobody said the word "witch" and no female hung by the seat of her skirt or fell from a tree. On New Year's Eve, 1945, Joe Breen, after reviewing the rewrite, sent his various concerns: "Avoid any offense" to newspapermen; "tone down the various gruesome angles of the story"; "suggest the choking out of scene."

There was also some concern about a character called "Kyra Goran," but more about her later.

The assigned director was Erle C. Kenton, Universal workhorse whose genre credits boasted Paramount's *Island of Lost Souls* (1932) and Universal's *The Ghost of Frankenstein* (1942). More recently, he'd helmed Universal's "monster rallies," *House of Frankenstein* (1944) and *House of Dracula* (1945).

The Cat Creeps had a 12-day schedule—and a budget of $144,060. This was 18 days less than the schedules for *House of Frankenstein* or *House of Dracula*, and the budget was

Pressbook ballyhoo exhibitors showing suggested publicity stunt for the double bill of *She-Wolf Of London* and *The Cat Creeps*.

more than $200,000 less than each of those two "monster-rally" shockers.

Kenton's fee for *The Cat Creeps*: $5,000.

The pressbook for *The Cat Creeps* claimed the film concerned a cat possessed by the devil, but no such luck. Suffice to say, the tepid mystery yarn all takes place on a full moon night in a spooky old house called "Key Towers" on an eerie island. Three people die before the murderer is revealed; one of them, tripped by

Fred Brady and Noah Beery, Jr. in the newspaper office.

the villain, falls on a pitchfork. Blackmail and a hidden stash of money spike the plot.

It wasn't much to run with.

Thursday, January 3, 1946: The Cat Creeps began shooting on Stage 20. The cinematographer was George Robinson, who'd filmed many of Universal's horror shows, including *House of Frankenstein* and *House of Dracula.*

The set was the interior editor's office. On call that morning was the top-billed Noah Beery, Jr., who played "Flash," a newspaper photographer. In the movie, his nickname is "Pidge," which was Beery's actual nickname ... and which suggests a certain informality reigned over the shoot. Beery, who'd later won his top fame as James Garner's Dad on TV's *The Rockford Files,* was on contract to Universal in 1946 and received a flat salary for *The Cat Creeps* of $4,000.

Playing "Terry Nichols," heroic reporter, was strapping, pompadoured Fred Brady. Although he was the film's lead, his salary for *The Cat Creeps* was set at $1,700. He later became a prolific TV writer on shows such as *Four-Star Playhouse, Colt .45,* and *77 Sunset Strip*; he also wrote the screenplay for *Champagne for Caesar* (1950), featuring one of Vincent Price's best comic performances.

Beery and Brady worked on the editor's office set with William Davidson, Arthur Loft and Terry Jerome, as well as 10 extras. Neither the three men in the office nor the 10 extras are ever seen again in the movie.

At 1:00 p.m., Lois Collier, Universal contract star of such films as Maria Montez's *Cobra Woman* and Acquanetta's *Jungle Woman,* reported for her call to begin playing heroine Gay Elliott. Her salary: a flat $2,000 for the picture. Shooting moved to the Elliott house's hall and library sets on Stage 18.

It was a 100-page script and required shooting eight-and-a-half pages per day to meet the 12-day schedule. Today, Kenton had only shot seven and a half pages. *The Cat Creeps*, after day one, was one page behind schedule.

Friday, January 4: Joining the show was Jonathan Hale, who played Walter Elliott, Gay's father and was set to earn $2,000 for *The Cat Creeps.* Hale racked up over 240 film and TV credits in his career and had enjoyed running roles in two series: RKO's *The Saint* movies, and Columbia's *Blondie* pictures. Come 1966, however, and reportedly despondent, Hale fatally shot himself. An odd postscript: In 2013, 47 years after his death, a fan or fans placed a plaque over Hale's unmarked grave at Valhalla Memorial Park in North

Iris Clive holds Smoky, flanked by Noah Beery, Jr. (left), Douglass Dumbrille (right), and Paul Kelly (far right).

Hollywood, bearing his name, birth and death dates, the name "Mr. Dithers" (his character in the *Blondie* movies), and the words, "We remember you."

Come afternoon, Kenton and company moved from Stage 18 to Stage 9 for a scene in the office of McGalvey, lawyer. Douglass Dumbrille, veteran Hollywood villain, played McGalvey, who turns out (Spoiler Alert!) to be the mystery killer. His salary for *The Cat Creeps*: $2,000. Dum-

brille would raise eyebrows in Hollywood in 1960, when, at age 70, he married 28-year-old Patricia Mowbray, daughter of actor Alan Mowbray—who was almost seven years younger than Dumbrille.

Reporting that afternoon was Rose Hobart, as Connie, a doomed blackmailer. She'd played Muriel in Paramount's 1931 *Dr. Jekyll and Mr. Hyde* and had acted in various other horror films as well, notably as the Devil herself in Columbia's

Fred Brady, Noah Beery, Jr. and Paul Kelly investigate outdoors.

Murder! Noah Beery, Jr., Douglass Dumbrille, Rose Hobart, Lois Collier, Jonathan Hale, and Paul Kelly observe as Fred Brady finds the body of Vera Lewis in this tense moment from *The Cat Creeps*.

1944 *Soul of a Monster*. Her salary for *The Cat Creeps*: $1,667. She later ran afoul of the Hollywood Witch Hunt and was blacklisted for many years.

The day ended at 6:10 p.m. Kenton had shot eight pages, not the required eight and a half.

Saturday, January 5: The company shot exterior scenes at Universal's Concrete Tank, as well as the Shelby Woods on the back lot and the Boat Landing set on Stage 15. Joining the cast: Paul Kelly, who was paid $4,000 for *The Cat Creeps*. Kelly was a fine actor who'd somehow lived down the fact that, in 1927, he'd beaten to death Ray Raymond, a Ziegfeld song-and-dance man, who was the husband of Kelly's lover, actress Dorothy Mackaye. In what might have made a hot pre-Code melodrama, Kelly paid off a doctor to fake the cause of death, but the coroner, acting on a tip, claimed the body just before it could be cremated and demanded an autopsy. Kelly was convicted of manslaughter, Mackaye was convicted of conspiracy, and both served time at San Quentin. After they were released, Kelly and Mackaye married in 1931. (Dorothy Mackaye died in a car accident in 1940.)

In 1947, Kelly would star in Broadway's *Command Decision*, playing the role Clark Gable later played in the 1948 MGM film, and would win a Tony award. By the way, the house where the fatal beat-ing took place is still in the guidebooks: 2261 Cheremoya, Hollywood Hills.

Work on *The Cat Creeps* ended that Saturday at 6:30 p.m. Possibly due to the exterior scenes, shot both on a set and on the back lot, Kenton only completed four and a half pages.

Monday, January 7. It was a new week, and day four of *The Cat Creeps*. The call was at 1:00 p.m. due to shooting scheduled that night. Lois Collier, Fred Brady, Noah Beery, Jr., Douglass Dumbrille, Rose Hobart, and Jonathan Hale acted that afternoon on Stage 15. Joining them for its first day of shooting: the black cat, named Smoky.

As it was, Smoky had a problem with film technique. Fascinated by the over-hanging microphone, the cat stared at it, rather than at its trainer. Catnip provided at the right time and in the right places saved the day.

Smoky was done at 4:30 p.m. but the human cast worked after dinner on Universal's back lot, specifically by "Lubin Lake," whose banks represented the Key Towers Landing and Grounds. Shooting ended at 10:40 p.m. Kenton had shot five and a quarter pages.

(By this time, Kenton probably realized what a turkey he had on his hands. The director likely wished he could have recalled one of his beast men from *Island of Lost Souls* and have him run half-naked through Key Towers, scaring the hell out of everybody.)

Tuesday, January 8: Work focused on the Mrs. Williams Room set on Stage 15. Joining the company as "Mrs. Williams" was an actress who'd screamed in *King Kong*. No, it wasn't Fay Wray ... it was 72-year-old Vera Lewis, who had let loose a scream as an audience member in *King*

Iris Clive, Paul Kelly, and Rose Hobart—all of whom had colorful real-life Hollywood sagas to tell—manage to look intensely involved in the lackluster goings-on of *The Cat Creeps*. Once again Ms. Clive is holding Smoky.

Kong's theater sequence. As the deranged hag terrified in Key Towers, Vera Lewis provided a few mild shivers. The cat worked 9 to 5, and Paul Kelly and Rose Hobart were the last to leave the set at 6:30 p.m. Kenton had shot eight pages.

Wednesday, January 9: The same players worked on the same set. So did Smoky. Vera Lewis wrapped up her role—her character expired. The actress had earned $500. Kenton had his best day yet as far as coverage—he shot nine and a quarter pages.

Thursday, January 10: *The Cat Creeps* welcomed a new player, who was billing herself at this time as "Iris Clive." She was Iris Lancaster, and she'd been the lover of Colin Clive, portrayer of the title role in Universal's 1931 *Frankenstein*.

A leggy redhead who'd capered as a showgirl in such films as *Flying Down to Rio* (RKO, 1934) and *Murder at the Vanities* (Paramount 1934), Iris Lancaster had met Clive circa 1934, and a passionate romance followed. They never married—he had a wife back in England—but Iris was devoted, and at the end of his life, lived with him in his house high in Hollywood's Los Feliz colony. She also oversaw his funeral arrangements and cremation after his death on June 25, 1937.

Iris hadn't won any notable film success. Come the mid-1940s, she was working in Westerns and had taken—presumably in homage to her late lover—the professional name of "Iris Clive." She signed on for *The Cat Creeps* at a total salary of $375, the lowest-paid principal in the cast. What she lost in money, she gained in presence. As Kyra Goran, Iris has the flashiest role in the film—an alluring, mysterious "Cat Woman," carrying the black cat, fondling it to her bosom, speaking in a foreign accent, acting as if performing a lampoon of Simone Simon in Val Lewton's *Cat People*—or, more precisely, Elizabeth Russell, the original "Cat Woman" in that 1942 classic.

"Within this cat," she purrs in a foreign accent, "is the spirit of my friend, Mrs. Williams!"

And lampoon is right. It turns out that "Kyra Goran" was a stripper in the Follies, hired to help snare the killer. The revelation is rather along the lines of Carroll Borland's "Luna" in *Mark of the Vampire* (MGM, 1935), although *The Cat Creeps* tips off the audience before the climax that Kyra is in cahoots with the hero. This character inspired Joseph Breen to address two concerns in assessing *The Cat Creeps* censorable script elements:

Page 95: Kyra's speech, "Honey, an actress is anything for a price," should be changed to

One could tune in TV's *Shock! Theatre* on the right night and see *The Black Cat* starring Boris Karloff and Bela Lugosi. On the wrong night, *Shock! Theatre* might offer *The Cat Creeps*, starring Fred Brady and Noah Beery, Jr.

something along the line of, "An actress will take any part for a price."

Page 99: scenes 309, 310: Please delete or change the present suggestion that Kyra is getting ready to do a bump. We could approve the suggestion of a fan dance at this point, which should not be handled objectionably."

There's no "bump" or "fan dance," but Iris Clive nicely puts over her racy character, nonetheless.

(A question comes to mind about Iris Clive and *The Cat Creeps*: Did the actress cite her relationship with Colin Clive when she tried out for the part ... thinking it might impress the casting director that she'd once been the mistress of "Henry Frankenstein"?)

Kenton shot eight and a quarter pages today. He was seven days through the 12-day shoot. The assistant director *Daily Report* noted that the director had shot 50 and three quarters pages of the script, and he had 49 and a quarter left to do.

Friday, January 11: All the principals worked on Stage 15 from 9:00 a.m. to 6:20 p.m. As this was a long day for Smoky, at least two cats tackled the role.

Saturday, January 12: The principals (except for Rose Hobart, who wasn't on call) and "cats" again acted on Stage 15. It was a long, productive day, and Kenton shot 10 and a quarter pages. Last to go at 7:35 p.m. were Iris Clive and the cats.

Monday, January 14: Elwood Bredell (veteran Universal cinematographer, whose credits included *The Ghost of Frankenstein*) replaced George Robinson as cameraman, and there were several other changes on the crew as well. Rose Hobart was back, and the eight players worked on the same set as they had on Saturday. Kenton shot seven pages. Once again, the last to go home at 6:30 p.m. were Iris Clive and the cats.

(By the way, Universal started shooting that day the serial *Lost City of the Jungle*, the studio's second-to-last serial, and the final screen work of Lionel Atwill. The venerable horror star was too ill to complete it, was replaced by a double, and died April 22.)

Tuesday, January 15: Seven of the principals, as well as the cats, were on call at 9:00 a.m. Iris Clive reported at noon. Kenton filmed seven and three quarter pages. Hobart, Hale, and Iris Clive wrapped up the day at 6:35 p.m. ... with the cats.

Wednesday, January 16. The Cat Creeps was supposed to finish shooting this day, but 12 days is very little time to shoot a movie, and when Fred Brady, Noah Beery, Jr., Jonathan Hale, Iris Clive—and the cats—went home at 6:35 p.m., there were still nine and a half pages to shoot.

Thursday, January 17: Lois Collier, Fred Brady, Noah Beery, Jr., Douglass Dumbrille, Jonathan Hale, Iris Clive, and

A foreign movie poster for *The Cat Creeps* ... trying hard to entice horror fans!

Maybe if enough cast members scream in the movie, the audience will assume *The Cat Creeps* is actually scary.

the cats performed their final scenes on the Cellar and "Tag Room" sets on Stage 15. Kenton shot the remaining nine and a half pages.

The production closed at 7:30 p.m. The film had come in one day over schedule and almost precisely on budget. Paul Sawtell would add the musical score that featured feline-sounding flourishes.

It was a season of change at Universal City. On January 22, five days after *The Cat Creeps* finished up, the studio began shooting its final Sherlock Holmes mystery, *Dressed to Kill*, starring Basil Rathbone, Nigel Bruce, and Patricia Morison.

Thursday, April 4: Universal, planning to double-bill *The Cat Creeps* with *She-Wolf of London* (starring June Lockhart and Don Porter, and shot in December of 1945), previewed both films at the studio. *Variety* tried to toss *The Cat Creeps* a bone:

...a straight mystery which qualifies for second billing ... Erle C. Kenton makes the most of

a sometimes-careless script ... Miss Collier makes a pretty heroine ... Iris Clive is in for an interesting bit ...

Friday, May 17: *The Cat Creeps* played as a solo at New York City's horror salon, the Rialto Theatre. The *New York Times* titled its review "Puss in Boots" and critiqued that, while "The cat gives a pretty good performance," it received only "mediocre support" from the humans in the film. *Variety* reported that *The Cat Creeps* "clawed its way to a nice $9,100" at the Rialto, but it wasn't held over for a second week.

The pressbook for *She-Wolf of London* and *The Cat Creeps* offered this exploitation ballyhoo to lure audiences:

You can get a cat costume from your local costumer, and perhaps a local mask maker could lend his talents in fashioning a good cat head. The woman who impersonates the She-Wolf of London can wear a veil to hide her features and at the same time create a mysterious effect ...

Send the two people around town together a few days before your opening! ... They carry a banner between them that reads, "We're the terror twins in the double horror show She-Wolf of London *and* The Cat Creeps *...!"*

In a little over 15 years, Universal horror, having thrived through the Depression and World War II, had expired with a mellow "meow."

When *Shock! Theatre* came to TV in the fall of 1957, *The Cat Creeps*, as part of the package, must have seemed incongruous. After a horror fan had beheld

Lugosi's Dracula, Karloff's Frankenstein Monster, and Chaney's Wolf Man, what was Smoky the Cat supposed to do to his pulse?

One also wonders: Did Iris Clive (who'd gone through an ugly divorce in the early 1950s and whose career was by then over) tune in to see herself slink through *The Cat Creeps?* And did she stay up to see her tragic, long-ago lover in *Frankenstein?* (She died in 2001. For much more on Iris Lancaster, read my book *One Man Crazy! The Life and Death of Colin Clive*).

While *The Cat Creeps* dropped the curtain on Universal horror with a resounding thud, it's nevertheless a part of the studio's special legacy, filmed on those same hallowed grounds where the classics had taken on an eerie immortality. In the glory days, 1934 specifically, Universal had diabolically exalted a cat in *The Black Cat*, co-starring Karloff and Lugosi. While that shocker had screeched, howled, and clawed, the best *The Cat Creeps* ever whipped up was a moody purr.

Yet, it's "a part of the family"—and as such, deserves, however unworthy, a certain acceptance ... and maybe even affection.

(Greg Mank's new book Angels and Ministers of Grace Defend Us! More Dark Alleys of Classic Horror Cinema *is set for June 2022 publication by McFarland. Please visit his website at www.gregorymank.com, for more news and information.)*

BY JIM NEMETH

ROBERT BLOCH
MORE THAN JUST
THE "AUTHOR OF PSYCHO"

Alfred Hitchcock's classic film *Psycho* was an enormous financial success upon its release in 1960. Based upon the novel of the same name by Robert Bloch, the film's success spilled over into the author's life as well. Sales of the book skyrocketed with demand resulting in numerous printings and publication in numerous languages. The most significant effect on Bloch's life, however, was the creation of a permanent and unshakable association between the author and what became his literary "Frankenstein Monster." For Bloch would forever after be known as "The Author of Psycho," a label that would stick with the writer and accompany practically everything that bore his

name, until his passing in 1994—and beyond. Sadly, the ever-present specters of Norman Bates and his maternal alter ego overshadowed all the author's post-*Psycho* accomplishments. For it was the rare interview or other media event where discussion would not inevitably turn from Bloch's latest project to some aspect of *Psycho*—be it film, book, or inspiration.

With invariable good grace, Bloch eventually came to accept, if not necessarily embrace, his *psycho*tic

association and the baggage that came with it.

I, however, have not. With this article, I hope to provide a glimpse into the breadth of Robert Bloch's versatility as a writer—the author of over 25 novels, hundreds of short stories and numerous scripts for radio, television, and film. While most prolific in the worlds of fantasy and horror, Bloch was equally adept at writing thrillers, science fiction, detective/crime, Westerns and even slapstick humor.

So, let us explore the diverse career of a man who is much more than just

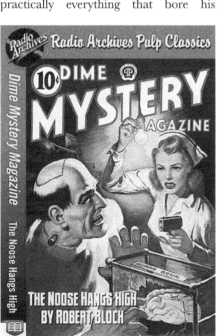

A late-in-life portrait of Robert Bloch

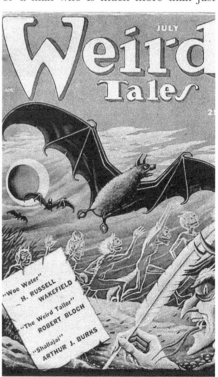

the author of one novel adapted into a cinematic classic.

SHORT STORIES

The seed of Bloch's writing career was sown in 1927 when his aunt purchased his first copy of *Weird Tales* magazine. The young Bloch thrilled to the bizarre and fantastic tales contained within and over the years came to particularly favor those of (the now) renowned writer, H.P. Lovecraft. Bloch wrote a fan letter to Lovecraft in 1933. Lovecraft responded, to Bloch's surprise, shortly thereafter, and thus began an ongoing correspondence that continued until Lovecraft's death in 1937. Initially, the senior author encouraged Bloch to try his hand at story writing and later provided welcome encouragement and feedback to the youthful Bloch's submissions.

Bloch's efforts quickly met with success. He first saw publication in 1934 in the fantasy and horror 'zines, *Marvel Tales,* and *Weird Tales.* The latter publication, originally merely a source of unending entertainment to a young boy's dark imagination, in later years practically became Bloch's literary "home" until the magazine's demise in the mid-1950s. Much of Bloch's early work emulated Lovecraft's style and subject matter, often employing the use of Lovecraft's Cthulhu Mythos, an elaborate fictional universe dominated by the titular deity, the monstrous Cthulhu, who once reigned over the Earth. Although long since banished, Cthulhu remains worshiped by a cult of zealous followers who believe in, and work toward, his eventual return.

It wasn't until the early 1940s that Bloch began to move away from his Lovecraftian influences and find his own voice. His fiction, which to date had primarily explored the realms of the fantastic and supernatural, began to take a new direction. The author now began to turn his focus inward, looking to exploit the limitless terrors inherent within the human animal.

Given his new predilection for writing tales detailing the atrocities spawned from the abnormal mind, it's not surprising that Bloch maintained a keen interest in the life and mythos surrounding real-life serial killer Jack the Ripper. Bloch featured the infamous slasher frequently in his work, first broaching the subject in his classic 1943 story, "Yours Truly, Jack the Ripper." Bloch revisited the character in two subsequent short stories, "A Most Unusual Murder" and "A Toy for Juliette," his contribution to Harlan Ellison's famed 1967 story collection *Dangerous Visions,* as well as the teleplay "Wolf in the Fold" (1967) for the original *Star Trek* television series.

While the succeeding decades would see Bloch branch out into different mediums, he never stopped writing stories. When *Weird Tales* ceased publication in 1954, Bloch's tales continued to find homes in such disparate mainstream and genre publications such as *Amazing, Ellery Queen's Mystery Magazine, Shock, Mammoth Westerns, Twilight Zone Magazine,* and *Playboy.* His voluminous output was regularly collected and published, approaching 50 collections. Of note, in 1959, Bloch's short, "That Hellbound Train," won the Hugo Award (an annual literary award for the best science fiction works and achievements of the previous year), which forever amused the author for being a straight-out "deal-with-the-devil" fantasy tale.

RADIO

Bloch spent little time working within the medium. Aside from writing radio scripts in 1940 in support of Milwaukee

political candidate Carl Zeidler's bid for mayor, Bloch's only commercial foray into radio broadcasting came in 1945, with the debut of *Stay Tuned for Terror.* A program devoted to horror and the supernatural in the same vein as *Lights Out, Terror's* initial and only season, featured 39, 15-minute radio plays. The scripts, all written by Bloch, consisted of eight originals, with the remainder adapted from his own stories, primarily from *Weird Tales,* who promoted the radio show within their pages. Sadly, this radio program is for the most part "lost," with exception of two episodes that have only recently been discovered.

NOVELS

With his turn in the early 1940s to mining the psychology and inner workings of the human brain for material, Bloch brought a level of realism to his work that was more chilling for now hitting close to home—for the monster in the room was no longer the vampire or ghoul of old, but it could well be the very person standing next to you. Bloch's first published novel, *The Scarf* (1947), expanded upon this theme and established his unique take on literary psychological horror—that of telling his story from the first-person perspective of the villain/antagonist. Bloch would use this effective and lauded technique again in subsequent novels *The Will to Kill* and *The Kidnaper* (sic), both 1954. (It should be noted, that while far from being the first to use the concept of the unreliable narrator in his fiction,

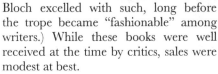

Alfred Hitchcock Presents ... "The Sorcerer's Apprentice"

Bloch excelled with such, long before the trope became "fashionable" among writers.) While these books were well received at the time by critics, sales were modest at best.

And then there was *Psycho*.

In 1959, Simon & Schuster published Bloch's magnum opus, *Psycho*. The book met with generally favorable reviews and was an instant hit with readers; its initial hardcover print run sold out quickly. It's important to note here that the novel was a considerable success on its own *before* Hitchcock's cinematic adaptation the following year. That the novel went on to even greater success after the film's release is undeniable, as related in our opening paragraph. But it's continually frustrating to read decades later "authoritative"

statements from persons who state (incorrectly) that Bloch's novel only became a success after the film's release.

That said, and with this article's stated purpose, we move on.

Bloch's post-*Psycho* novel work consists of nearly 20 books, stretching across the fields of science fiction, fantasy, psychological thrillers, crime/mystery, historical-based horror, screenplay novelizations and more. Of note, he revisited his most famous creation, Norman Bates, in two additional books, *Psycho II* (not the source for the film of the same name) and *Psycho House*. With noted science fiction author Andre Norton, he co-authored, *The Jekyll Legacy* (1990), a sequel to the Robert Louis Stevenson classic *Strange Case of Dr Jekyll and Mr Hyde*. The book was written in a most unusual fashion: writing alternate chapters in sequence. This entailed Bloch writing a chapter, sending it off to Norton, and then needing to wait for Norton's subsequent chapter to arrive before proceeding. In *American Gothic* (1974), he fictionalized the horrors of real-life serial killer H.H. Holmes, who brutally murdered young women during the 1893 Chicago World's Fair. Bloch was hired to write the novelization for the ill-fated *Twilight Zone: The Movie* (1983), although the resulting paperback did not provide him with a cover byline. Lastly, Bloch ended his long association with Jack the Ripper in 1984 with *The Night of the Ripper*. An acclaimed entry in the Ripper canon, the book is notable for weaving such real-life personages as Sir Arthur Conan Doyle, the Elephant Man and Oscar Wilde into

its storyline. An additional fascinating aspect of this novel, as related by the author himself in his autobiography *Once Around the Bloch*, "In order to underscore the point that throughout history, crimes far worse than Jack's had been committed in the name of patriotism, religion, local custom or tradition, I include a number of examples as chapter headings." Upon publication, as par for the course for reviewers, they missed the point and thought said examples were added merely to add excessive gore.

TELEVISION

Bloch's entrance into writing for television originated when friend Samuel Peeples—at the time a writer of Western teleplays for such series as *Wanted: Dead or Alive* and *The Rifleman*—requested Bloch to come to Hollywood to write a script for the crime drama, *Lock-Up*. Bloch's initial submission was accepted and led to additional assignments.

Bloch worked steadily in the medium throughout the 1960s and '70s, writing

Alfred Hitchcock Presents ... "The Cuckoo Clock" with Fay Spain and Beatrice Straight

William Shatner in "The Grim Reaper" episode of Boris Karloff's *Thriller*, written by Robert Bloch.

THE DEAD DON'T DIE

DOUGLAS S. CRAMER PRODUCTIONS Present
THE DEAD DON'T DIE
Starring GEORGE HAMILTON RAY MILLAND LINDA CRISTAL
JOAN BLONDELL and RALPH MEEKER
Written by ROBERT BLOCK Produced by HENRY COLMAN
Directed by CURTIS HARRINGTON

teleplays for numerous popular and acclaimed television series. With friends in the business introducing Bloch to executives and producers in the industry, he came to Universal Studios in late 1959 and met the staff producing *Alfred Hitchcock Presents*. Given that the show had produced two of Bloch's stories, they asked him to write a script, an adaptation of Frank Mace's "The Cuckoo Clock." Upon delivery of the script, he was offered subsequent assignments, ultimately writing a total of eight teleplays for *Presents*. Arguably the most notable of these was his own story, "The Sorcerer's Apprentice." This episode is (in)famous

Night Gallery ... the portrait used for the episode "Logoda's Heads."

for *not* being broadcast during the series' original run, for its ending being deemed too gruesome (the implication of Diana Dors being sawn in half). The episode later saw its debut on television when the series went into syndication. Bloch would continue to write for the show after its expansion to an hour in length and renamed *The Alfred Hitchcock Hour*.

During his Hitchcock tenures, he additionally became involved with writing for *Thriller* (1960-62), a new mystery/ suspense anthology series starring Boris Karloff as its host. Through this stint, Bloch first met the famed horror actor, which led to the pair becoming close friends. Bloch wrote a total of seven scripts for *Thriller*, many adaptations of his own stories. He adapted one story not his own, D.M. Lessing's "The Black Madonna," retitled "The Grim Reaper," starring William Shatner, which would come to be known as one of the more memorable episodes of the series.

For *Night Gallery*, Rod Serling's supernatural-leaning follow-up to his lauded *Twilight Zone*, Bloch sadly (if ever a show was geared toward his forte!), contributed only one entry, adapting August Derleth's 1939 short, "Logoda's Heads." Invited to write a script for the original *Star Trek*, Bloch ultimately contributed three teleplays: the light-weight

entries "Catspaw" and "What are Little Girls Made Of?" as well as the previously mentioned nod to the Ripper, "Wolf in the Fold." Here, Bloch transforms "Red Jack" into a non-corporeal entity who takes over the Enterprise's computer, and thus, control of the ship, before Kirk and Spock save the day.

Bloch additionally wrote the teleplays for two major network "Movies of the Week"—*The Cat Creature* (1973) and *The Dead Don't Die* (1975), the former an original story, the latter an adaptation of Bloch's own story. Both films were directed by Curtis Harrington, a writer and director of primarily low-budget horror and science-fiction films (*Night Tide*, *How Awful About Allan*, etc.). *Cat Creature* was meant as an homage to the spirit of the Val Lewton classic, *Cat People* (1942), while *Dead* concerns itself with zombies shambling the streets of Chicago in the 1930s. Neither project left Bloch and Harrington completely satisfied, due to typical corporate and network intrusion into the scripts.

MOTION PICTURES

Bloch's entry into writing feature films came in 1962 when his agent procured the gig of writing the screenplay for *The Couch*. Based on a treatment by Blake "*Breakfast at Tiffany's*" Edwards, the psychological horror film was much in line with Bloch's novels of the 1950s, in that it explored the inner workings of a disturbed

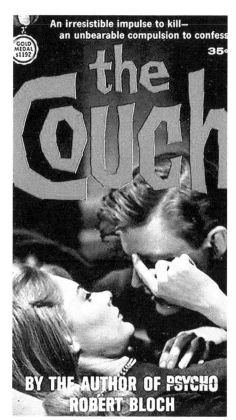

killer. Due to budgetary constrictions, much of what Bloch wanted to visualize on screen involving his main character's hallucinations was cut, resulting in a static, dull affair that went nowhere and faded quickly. After writing the first draft for a proposed remake/reimagining of the silent classic *The Cabinet of Dr. Caligari*, the film's director Roger Kay not only rewrote dialogue which destroyed Bloch's finely crafted plot, but Kay also attempted to steal the writing credit as well. (He failed.)

Later that same year, Bloch was approached by William Castle, the B-movie director known for promotion of his films using elaborate gimmicks. In *House on Haunted Hill* (1959) some theaters erected a pulley system near the theater screen which allowed a plastic skeleton to be flown over the audience, a process called EMERGO. In *The Tingler* (1959) electrical "buzzers" were attached to the underside of some theater seats to provide "tingling" sensations during certain scenes, a process to be called PERCEPTO! Writing about the idea of a latter-day Lizzie Borden-type axe murderess, Bloch wrote an original script for what would soon become *Strait-Jacket*. A huge boon for all concerned came when legendary Oscar-winner Joan Crawford agreed to star. Released in 1964, the film was panned by many critics, but was a considerable box-office hit.

Obviously happy with the result of their collaboration, Castle again turned to Bloch to write *The Night Walker*, another psychological thriller, this time starring Barbara Stanwyck (*Stella Dallas*, *The Big Valley*) in her final film role. Receiving mixed reviews, *Walker* did not match the success of its predecessor, and Castle and Bloch would not collaborate again.

In 1965, Bloch was approached by producers Milton Subotsky and Max Rosenberg, recent founders of the British film production company Amicus, to pen a film that became *The Psychopath*. While this film and a subsequent assignment, *The*

Deadly Bees, adapted from Gerald Heard's *A Taste for Honey*, went nowhere at the box-office, these films led to an extended and successful collaboration with Subotsky and Rosenberg. In 1967, the pair released *Torture Garden*, a horror anthology film whose four Bloch-scripted adaptations of his own stories are connected by a framing story. The film was a success and so the producers looked to the author to repeat the formula with two subsequent releases, *The House That Dripped Blood* (1971) and *Asylum* (1972). While both films were sizeable hits, regrettably the latter film proved to be Bloch's last produced film screenplay.

In the end, there is no denying the impact of Alfred Hitchcock's *Psycho* on Robert Bloch's career. It's only natural that any publisher or film/television producer would want to tie the film's enduring popularity to any artifact produced by Bloch. But while *Psycho* may have been his biggest success, it is unfair to have it define his entire career. Or legacy. As related, Bloch's output across seven decades was voluminous and spanned many mediums—with the author experiencing success in each. While it is delightful to learn from Robert Bloch's daughter, that, "Dad would be pleased to know that he still has an amazingly large fan base, some of whom are astoundingly young," to the sadly uninitiated, the name Robert Bloch does not register unless the inevitable tagline "The Author of Psycho" is appended. It is my sincerest hope that this article serves as a small first step in reversing that

THE MIGHTY MILTON REID

BY CHRISTOPHER GULLO

When the word "henchman" is spoken, it usually conjures up images of a hulking figure capable of immense strength who does the bidding of some evil villain. Rip that person from the celluloid screen and you have Milton Reid—aka Jungle Boy, aka The Mighty Chang. With a 5-foot-11-inch height, 54-inch chest, 250-pound frame and downright mean foreign looks, Reid struck an impressive sight and as a result made a career out of playing heavies in both wrestling arenas and in film and television. Although sometimes cast as Chinese or Middle Eastern, Reid was in fact born in Bombay, India on April 29, 1917. His foreign looks were from the mix of his parents—his father was Edgar William Reid, a Scottish customs inspector who met and married an Indian woman from Bombay while stationed there.[1] Besides their son Milton Rutherford Reid, they also had a daughter who remained in India with her mother. Reid would attend a British military school while in India where he de-

veloped, as has been described from those who worked with him, a very cultured voice.[2] Coincidentally this worked against Reid later in his career as producers and directors would feel that his voice did not match his massive frame, and so the characters he played would often be rendered mute or voiced-over by other actors. Following military school, Reid moved to England in 1936 and settled in Shepherd's Bush at 7 Tadmore Street. When World War II broke out, Reid joined the British army and served the entire length of the war as a gunner in the Royal Artillery.[3] Prior to serving in the military, Reid married Bertha Guyett, a fashion artist, in 1939. The couple had a son, Milton Reid, Jr, born in 1941.

Following several years working as a commercial traveler, Reid decided to use his large physical build to his advantage and entered the world of professional wrestling. Although he was 35 years old, in 1952, by the time he broke into the wrestling business, Reid's new given ring

persona was the youthful sounding Jungle Boy. His character's backstory was simply that he was the son of an Indian forestry official and as a child the jungle was his playground.[4] As a heavyweight who sported leopard skin trunks with his hair tied back tightly, Reid was soon wrestling all over Northern England and Scotland at such places as the Belle Vue Manchester and St James Hall, where he battled against other heavyweights including Dennis Mitchell, Joe Zaranoff and Billy Joyce. Not a technical wrestler, Reid relied on his size and strength to use power moves to defeat his opponents in the ring. His larger-than-life persona eventually attracted the attention of film producers looking for a henchman for films and soon after Reid made his film debut as Mac, a goateed thug in the crime drama *Undercover Girl* (1958), retitled for the US markets as *Assignment Redhead*. Directed by Francis Searle for Butcher's Film Distributors, *Undercover Girl* was typical B movie fare—an enjoyable romp through

"I'll kill every man, woman and child in this camp –if my country loses the WAR!"

THE CAMP ON BLOOD ISLAND

CARL ANDRE EDWARD WALTER
MOHNER MORELL UNDERDOWN FITZGERALD

PHIL BROWN · BARBARA SHELLEY · MICHAEL GOODLIFFE

MEGASCOPE

The "money" shot when Milton Reid is about to hack off a soldier's head from *The Camp on Blood Island.*

nese—although both he and Maitland hailed from India. This film would start a pairing of the two actors, who from then on would often be cast on opposing sides. With no shirt on and hulking in size over the emaciated British soldiers, Reid's Japanese soldier shoves one of the prisoners on his knees before beheading him with a long saber. The shocking image of Reid about to separate the soldier's head from his shoulders was the most suspenseful scene in the entire film, even though the

audiences did not see the proverbial head rolling. It was recreated on the poster and novelization art to heavily promote the atrocities shown in the film. With no spoken lines in the film, Reid was essentially a featured extra, which would explain his lack of screen credit. Most likely, he was not even paid extra for his likeness used to advertise the film, but it certainly helped to put his face in the public spotlight and further his career. Other films would also capitalize on Reid's villainous looks in

the underworld of London complete with drug dealing Soho gangsters. While on the set, Reid made friends with actor Tony Quinn and the two men played chess when not filming.[5]

The same year Reid's next film would not even give him a name credit, but his image, in a notorious beheading scene was featured on the theater posters promoting *The Camp on Blood Island.* Made by Hammer Film Productions, better known for their Gothic horror films, *The Camp on Blood Island* was a brutal exploitative war drama playing out against the horrors of World War II. It starred André Morell and was directed by Val Guest. In the film, Reid played a Japanese soldier (goatee again) acting as the muscle for the sadistic Captain Sakamura, played by Marne Maitland. Producers felt Reid's foreign looks would pass well for Japa-

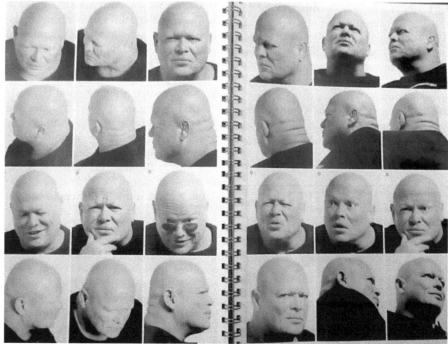

Reid poses for the *Fairborn Faces and Heads* visual reference books.

Milton Reid (left) in *Ferry to Hong Kong*

Reid's big break in film, resulting in his new wrestling persona, almost didn't occur. The producers of *Ferry to Hong Kong* had initially hired the seven-foot-tall Chang Ying Woo (one of Chinese nationalist leader Chiang Kai Shek's standard bearers) to play the Chinese pirate who could tower over the film stars Curt Jurgens and Orson Welles, who both topped over six feet. But when Woo arrived at the Hong Kong film set, his height proved to be too much for the camera, leading producers to continue their search and pick Reid instead.[8] The film is part adventure, part pseudo-comedy, thanks to the odd couple combination of Curt Jurgens as a ne'er-do-well named Conrad and Orson Welles as an uptight and not quite honest Captain Hart. Conrad winds up confined to Hart's ship after being expelled from Hong Kong due to poor behavior. The two men have an instant dislike for each other and after a near wreck of the ship and drifting out at sea, the ship is boarded by pirates. Marching on board from a Chinese junk is Johnny Sing-Up (Roy Chiao), a well-dressed pirate who introduces his new partner—a vulgar man of action called Yen (Milton Reid). As Yen, Reid had one of his largest film roles (clocking in at 16 minutes of screen time), which also allowed him dialogue.

their advertising poster art, and years later, Reid would even pose for the *Fairburn Faces and Heads* visual reference books.

Following a role as an executioner who hammers a massive stake through the heart of the titled count of *Blood of the Vampire* (credited this time, although his last name was misspelled as "Reed"), Reid's next film role in the Pinewood Studios production *Ferry to Hong Kong* (1959) would mark a distinctive change in his look which would stay with him for the rest of his career—a clean shaven head. This new look coincided with Reid's Jungle Boy persona losing a wrestling match to British heavyweight champion Bartolomeo "Bert" Assirati. Reid would reemerge on the wrestling scene as the villain known as The Mighty Chang hailing from the island of Sumatra.[6] His bald pate gave Reid imposing look which he sported for the remainder of his film roles. There is certainly a similarity here to another

wrestler turned actor—Tor Johnson. Johnson, who wrestled as Tor Johnson or the Super Swedish Angel, had shaved his head to give a more villainous look and would go on to appear in numerous B films and some Z film fare like *Plan 9 from Outer Space* for director Ed Wood. Looking back years later, however, Reid made himself out to be a trendsetter, "The trouble is that I originally shaved my head for a film, and everybody copied it and cashed in."[7] Reid's new persona was most likely due to the influence of Paul Lincoln, one of the most popular wrestlers in England who wore a mask wrestling under the moniker of Doctor Death. Lincoln ran his own wrestling promotion which Reid was part of and promoted his wrestlers at Granada Cinemas giving them colorful names and background stories to attract audiences. Seeing Reid portraying various Asian thugs in films, Lincoln probably saw a new way to promote his star and revive his wrestling career. Reid's Mighty Chang character was introduced September 20, 1960, with the nickname "The Asian Assassin" in a match against Gipsy Benito. With his new look, character and finishing move, the Sumatran Death Hold, Reid's notoriety grew, and he was soon grappling with the top draws in Paul Lincoln's promotion. Besides wrestling the likes of Iron Head Tarres, Rebel Ray Hunter and Judo Al Hayes, Reid's film roles increased in the 1960s, and he would alternate between wrestling and acting.

An Italian poster for *Ferry to Hong Kong*

The introduction of Reid's character of Yen also signals a change in the film. Up until this point the story is more of a loose comedy which turns serious and dramatic with his appearance. Even before Reid appears onscreen, his imposing figure is revealed in the eyes of Welles who first hears his heavy footsteps before his eyes widen in trepidation at seeing Yen approach. Sporting a long scar down the right side of his face, slanted eyes thanks to the makeup department and his newly

Milton Reid sends Richard Basehart through a door in *Visa to Canton*.

shaven bald head, Reid looked every bit the part of a ruthless Chinese pirate. Adopting an Asian accent, Reid's character barks out orders and threats alike and is quick to pull out his pistol or a knife when his demands aren't met fast enough. After forcing the ship's crew and passengers below deck, Yen spots a group of school children and decides to hold them for ransom. Yen is one of the more vicious characters portrayed by Reid; he thinks nothing of having a coffin ripped open in front of mourners as he looks for smuggled riches. When it is revealed that there was a body in the coffin, he angrily orders the body thrown overboard to the dismay of the mourners. Reid's ability to convey the intimidation of Yen using dialogue is also believable. In broken English with an Asian accent, Reid is constantly threatening and demanding—quickly telling everyone on the ship, "If you resist, you die." Even his partner Sing-Up tries to reason with him but has no effect on Yen's brutality. A crew member who unwisely punches Yen in the face has no effect other than the bullet Yen shoots, ending his life. Eventually Conrad schemes to retake

the ship by doing away with the threat of Yen; he angers and tricks Yen to walk in front of the ship's furnace which he has opened resulting in the villain being fried alive. Reid's physicality and notorious wrestling reputation apparently led to the elimination of a planned scene in the film. Director Lewis Gilbert explained that Curt Jurgens was supposed to be slapped by Reid's character in one scene, but the star was not keen on doing it. Reid revealed, "Yeah, it was a pity ... I would have loved to slap him ... for the sake of the picture of course."[9] A year later, Reid would once again play a Chinese pirate in Disney's *Swiss Family Robinson*. In this film Reid's pirate meets his end being run over by multiple rolling logs on a hillside while trying to attack the Robinson family. A standout among the other Chinese pirates, Reid was once again featured in the poster art for the film.

In the first of back-to-back Hammer Film Productions appearances, Reid played the uncredited Asian bodyguard of a Russian colonel played by Eric Pohlmann in the 1960 spy drama *Visa to Canton*. He speaks very few words besides denying the film's hero—a pilot named Don Benton played by Richard Basehart—entry into his boss' office. The pilot tries pushing the bodyguard out of the way which proves to be a big mistake. Reid decks him and the pilot crashes through the door onto the floor—he ar-

rives before the Russian colonel. Reid's bodyguard pops up again at the finale of the film, discovering his boss has been shot dead and pursues the responsible pilot through the back alleys of China before another gunfight ensues and this time Reid's character is dead on the ground. Marne Maitland also pops up in the film as an antiques dealer who is secretly helping the Chinese refugees.

The 1961 Hammer Film Production thriller *The Terror of The Tongs* featured

Milton Reid (left) and Christopher Lee (right) in *The Terror of The Tongs*

Milton Reid receives an ax to the neck in *The Terror of The Tongs.*

Reid as the uncredited servant of Red Dragon Tong gang leader, Chung King, played by Christopher Lee. Reid's character stands around shirtless looking intimidating most of the time until Chung King orders him to persuade a British captain, played by Geoffrey Toone, to give up information by scraping his bones with a needle. The torture scene is quite intense and horrifying with Reid giving steadfast determination along with an unnerving slight smile as he does his work. The captain passes out and is later freed by a Chinese village beggar and resistance fighter played by Marne Maitland, who swears revenge against the Tong. Reid's servant intervenes before their escape and he and Maitland's beggar do battle. During the fight Reid displays some of his wrestling moves, including an arm twist flip, rolling flip and a body slam before being done in by his own hatchet courtesy of the captain.

Later in 1961, Reid returned to the role of a swashbuckling pirate—both as a regular in the ITV costume dramatic series *Sir Francis Drake* and in his last film for Hammer—*Captain Clegg*. Already experienced in the role thanks to his part in *Swiss Family Robinson*, Reid secured a recurring role in *Sir Francis Drake*, the only recurring role he had during his acting career. Shown in the U.S. in 1962 as *The Adventures of Sir Francis Drake*, the series starred Terence Morgan in the title role and Jean Kent as Queen Elizabeth I; it was a historical adventure series with Drake and his crew exploring distant lands. The series had high production values as evidenced by the building of a full-size working replica of Drake's ship *The Golden Hind*. Playing one of Drake's men Diego, Reid started in the first episode "The Prisoner" and lasted for 15 episodes. He occasionally even got some lines—though mostly the "aye captain" or "yes master" gruff-voice variety.

Reid's most prominent role in the series was featured in the episode "Johnnie Factotum," in which Drake must go undercover into London's seedy underworld to uncover a nefarious plot and he takes along Diego as his muscle. Reid's best scene occurs in a tavern where all hell breaks loose involving Diego in an impromptu bar brawl with the equally large Chamberlain (Barry Shawzin), with spear

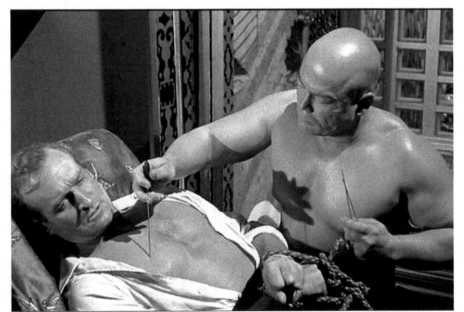

Geoffrey Toone and Milton Reid in the horrific torture scene in *The Terror of the Tongs*

Milton Reid with Terence Morgan in the *Sir Francis Drake* TV series.

throwing, knives and a man in a bear suit thrown in for good measure. Although the brawl is called off by Chamberlain's boss—their battle royal continues in the free-for-all climax in which Diego prevents Chamberlain from striking Drake with his sword and proceeds to pummel him into the ground. "Johnnie Factotum" also is notable in that it was directed by Peter Graham Scott, who later that year would be filming another swashbuckler tale—this time for Hammer—*Captain Clegg*. Michael Crawford, many years before his award-winning star turn in *Phantom of the Opera*, played John Drake in *Sir Francis Drake* and remembered Reid; "Milton had a red Thunderbird automobile, which everyone in the production was envious about, and they all wanted him to give them rides! I also remember Milton as being a very gentle giant."[10]

As Reid's involvement in *Sir Francis Drake* was that of a supporting player mostly swabbing the deck or doing his master's bidding, he most likely jumped at the chance to play the mulatto pirate in *Captain Clegg*. It wound up being the perfect time to literally jump ship as *Sir Francis Drake* did not last past the 1962 season. As director Peter Graham Scott was involved in both productions, it is reasonable to assume that he may have had a hand in recommending Reid for the role. *Captain Clegg*, known as *Night Creatures* in the US, was based on the Russell Thorndike's novel *Doctor Syn: A Tale of the Romney Marsh* and had been adapted to film as early as 1937 as *Doctor Syn*. Hammer had to change the name of Doctor Syn to Doctor Blyss as the Walt Disney Company owned the rights to Thorndike's Dr. Syn series of books and had their own version released the following year as *Dr. Syn, Alias the Scarecrow*.

Milton Reid takes a hard punch from Peter Cushing as Captain Clegg from *Captain Clegg* (US title, *Night Creatures*).

Hammer's take on Thorndike's novel remained much the same apart from the name changes to stave off Disney's lawyers. Reid had an important role as the mulatto pirate although had no lines thanks to being rendered mute by having his tongue cut out for assaulting the wife of the dreaded pirate Nathaniel Clegg, played by Hammer star Peter Cushing. The film starts out in 1776 showing Reid's mulatto onboard Clegg's ship being read the crime he is charged with. After a brief and frantic protest, the mulatto pirate is quickly subdued, and the camera zooms in on his eyes filled with fear hearing his proposed punishment. Reid's mulatto is next shown on a deserted island tied to a post with blood dripping from his mouth after having his tongue cut out with a sign above him warning those who would betray Clegg. So starts a mortal feud between the two men that continues 16 years later in the English village of Dymchurch. The village is being investigated for smuggling alcohol by Captain Collier and his men along with the mulatto pirate whom he rescued and is now his slave. Apparently, the mulatto has a keen nose for alcohol (which most likely is what

got him into trouble in the first place with Clegg) and Collier uses him like a human bloodhound to find the hidden distillery. The villagers are led by a parson called Dr. Blyss, who is actually Clegg, in disguise in order to avoid the English authorities. Reid's mulatto recognizes Blyss as his former pirate boss Clegg and, while not able to talk due to having his tongue

Milton Reid is left for dead, having his tongue cut out, in *Captain Clegg*, an action he never forgets.

Milton Reid is chased by one lone horse rider in *Spartacus and the Ten Gladiators*.

removed, tries to attack Blyss on two different occasions, drawing the suspicion of Collier. The mulatto, thinking of a way to prove what he knows, breaks open the coffin of Clegg revealing it to be empty, further narrowing the focus on Dr. Blyss. After eventually being exposed by Collier as the wanted pirate, Clegg attempts to escape but once again crosses path with the mulatto and a deadly fight ensues. After a knock-down drag-out battle, the mulatto fatally wounds Clegg with a spear (much like his previous swashbuckling battle in *Sir Francis Drake*) before being killed when Clegg's assistant Mipps, played by Michael Ripper, shoots him. *Captain Clegg* gave Reid his biggest film role which also was vital to the story—one could argue if it wasn't for Reid's mulatto, Collier would never have found anything illegal going on in Dymchurch and Blyss/Clegg would have gone on undetected. Plus, Reid was able to inject some humanity into the mulatto; examples being when he tries to communicate his knowledge of Clegg to the soldiers and uses his expressive eyes upon recognizing Blyss.

Reid played an uncredited Chinese boxer on the wrong side of a sword wielded by Charlton Heston in the 1963 historic drama, *55 Days at Peking*. As part of a group responsible for killing white missionaries and Chinese Christians, Reid's boxer draws the ire of Heston's Major Matt Lewis, who turns a display

of showmanship by the Chinese consulate into a chance to embarrass them with his quick thinking … and sword. The Spanish/Italian co-production sword and sandal adventure *Gli Invincibili Dieci Gladiatori* (*Spartacus and the Ten Gladiators*) offered Reid a much better villain that year in playing Chimbro—a former slave turned soldier for corrupt Patrician Senator Varro, who hunts for Spartacus while conducting secret raids for which the gladiator is blamed. Looking very much like his wrestling persona The Mighty Chang, Reid's nasty brute was voiced-over and once again uncredited. However, Reid has a lot of action scenes battling the hero gladiator Rocca, played by muscleman Dan Vadis. While it seems none of Reid's wrestling matches are available to view, *Spartacus and the Ten Gladiators* certainly gives viewers a glimpse at what a wrestling match with the Mighty Chang must have looked like. Before meeting his demise by his own sword, Reid displays his wrestling ability against the hero using a leg lock takedown, head lock, and clotheslines to try and beat his opponent. Reid's best moment in the film however doesn't involve the hero at all but comes when he runs down his own master with a chariot while making his getaway. The Italian film productions certainly made the most of Reid's physical talents as he appeared as a whip-wielding gladiator in *Il Crollo di Roma* (*The Fall of Rome*) the same year. He

seemingly has the upper hand against the hero before losing his balance in a tug of war resulting in him propelling headfirst into a stone wall.

The 1963 film noir *Panic* saw another reunion of the *The Camp on Blood Island* duo of Milton Reid and Marne Maitland. This time however, instead of a brute Japanese soldier and his sadistic Captain, Reid and Maitland play a scary tenant and a vile hotel manager, respectively. Written and directed by John Gilling (*The Plague of the Zombies*, *The Reptile* and *The Mummy's Shroud*), *Panic* tells the tale of Janine Heinig (Janine Gray), a secretary who is knocked out during a London jewelry robbery in which her boss is killed. She comes to with no memory of the event and is now pursued by both the police and the robbers. Along the way she tries to hide out in a seedy hotel run by Mr. Lantern (Maitland). While in her new room, she is visited by Dan (Reid), who tries to charm her with homemade cigarettes and brandy. When she is soon after sexually attacked by Mr. Lantern after he finds out who she is, it is Reid who comes to her rescue—pulling the hotel manager off Gray and picking him up like a rag doll to physically remove him from the room. It was an unusual red herring role for Reid, who is convincing as both a possible menace and savior to the female star. What is also unique about this film is that Reid has a speaking role and viewers can hear his natural, very soft spoken and cultured voice. It is somewhat unsettling to hear Reid's actual voice coming out of his large frame. If one would close their eyes and just listen to Reid's voice, they would most likely imagine a much smaller or

Milton Reid with Maurice Evans in *I, Spy.*

slimmer man. It is understandable then, how many directors opted to not give Reid any spoken lines. Reid would appear once more with Maitland in a 1967 episode of *I, Spy*, this time acting as a Middle Eastern associate of an Arab leader who guns down Maitland's Arab businessman.

Reid kept busy during the early 1960s with television and film roles although he still was wrestling on a regular basis. Johnny Kincaid, former European wrestling heavyweight champion, recalled a memory of traveling with Reid to a wrestling event where they were both scheduled. "This old man traveled with Milton only once and I swore that I would never travel with him again, and here's the reason why. He picked me up in his convertible Cadillac outside of Shepherd's Bush station and it was a lovely day as we drove all the way down to Exeter with the top down. After the show, we went and got our fish and chips and then set off for home, but

the weather had changed, and it was now cloudy and much colder. I asked Milton to put the convertible top up, but he said he liked to breathe in the fresh air, and we drove all the way back to Shepherd's Bush with that top down and I was frozen. So that was the first and last time I ever traveled with the Mighty Chang!"[11]

One of Reid's best film associations would be with the 007 series playing henchmen in two films of the series, and thus allowing him to battle two different Bonds—Sean Connery and Roger Moore. In the very first 007 film, *Dr. No* (1962), Reid would have a small role as one of the guards for Dr. No played by Joseph Wiseman. Decked out in a military fatigue, Reid's guard gets to shove a gun in Bond's back and rough him up afterwards. Perhaps hoping to strike while the iron was hot, Reid heavily campaigned to play another henchman—Oddjob, in the 1964 Bond film *Goldfinger*. When Reid learned that the producers were considering Olympic medal winner and fellow wrestler Toshiyuki "Harold" Sakata, aka Tosh Togo, for the part a month before production was due to begin, he made a public challenge to Sakata to wrestle him for the role. As stated by Reid, "I know I should have had the part. It was made for me. I feel sure I have had more acting experience than Togo. I have wrestled all over the world and am perfectly willing to fight Togo anywhere, any time—winner to get the part."[12] In Reid's favor, Togo was not a member of British Equity as he was, and Eon Productions had to apply for a permit to use him. The unusual challenge made headlines in the newspapers, but the producers decided that since Reid

was already in a previous Bond film that they would go with Sakata and the proposed wrestling match did not take place. This was certainly a missed opportunity for Reid, as Oddjob turned out to be one of the most iconic of the 007 henchmen with his razor-sharp steel-rimmed bowler hat.

Had Reid gotten the role of Oddjob, it certainly would have helped pay the bills. In December of 1965 Reid was in Westminster County court on a summons for an unpaid debt to the Automobile Association that he acquired while working in Rome on a spy film. Reid owed £52 for repairs to his car, of which he explained to the judge, "I am unemployed at present and I'm not finding it easy to get film parts. When I received this bill while in Rome, I never thought I would be in a position where I couldn't pay the AA." After telling the judge he hoped to get wrestling engagements in January, Reid was allowed a repayment plan of 10 shillings a month.[13]

When producers saw him as a prototypical strongman/henchman and expressed interest, Reid was only too happy to be hired to play those roles and pay his bills by appearing in some similar spy adventure films following *Dr. No*. The Italian film Reid alluded to in his court case was the 1965 Italian spy film *Agente Z 55 missione disperata* aka *Desperate Mission*. Perhaps as a dig at his previous competitor Tosh Togo for the role of Oddjob in *Goldfinger*, Reid's character, dubbed by another actor, is named To-go in the film. Reid's character is the main threat to Agent 55

Dr. No (Joseph Wiseman), guard (Milton Reid) and James Bond (Sean Connery)

Milton Reid as the assassin in *Agent Z 55 missione disperata*

Surprised by a deadly choke hold, Milton Reid is victim to Bulldog Drummond (Richard Johnson) in *Deadlier Than the Male*.

played by Germán Cobos and during their all-out brawl in the film's finale, Togo is done in by a blow torch. Reid's James Bond connection was also promoted in his wrestling matches as when he fought Bobo Matu in 1966 at the Matrix Hall in Coventry.

A more thinly veiled Bond take-off of sorts was the 1967 spy film *Deadlier Than the Male*—which was based on the character Bulldog Drummond. However, the Drummond character was established before author Ian Fleming wrote his first James Bond novel in 1953 and the Bulldog Drummond film adaptations dated back to 1922 so one could argue the 007 series borrowed from Bulldog Drummond. Another connection was that star Richard Johnson who played Drummond in *Deadlier Than the Male* was director Terence Young's first choice to play James Bond in *Dr. No*. In the film Reid's character is named Chang—not a stretch considering it was also his wrestler persona name. As Chang, Reid's character had more to do than in the Bond films. His character, working for the wealthy Carl Petersen (Nigel Green), trains the deadly beauties as referred to by the film's title. He also clashes constantly with Drummond—an introductory handshake turns into an impromptu Judo match with Drummond getting the upper hand. Chang gets back at Drummond when he 'accidentally' pours hot tea on him while serving Petersen's guests. After Drummond proceeds to incessantly insult Chang a final battle be-

tween the two is staged on a life size chess board. Even armed with a sword, Chang still ends up on the losing side and this time done in by his own weapon thanks to Drummond. Reid would return as a temple guard in 007 spoof *Casino Royale* released shortly after *Deadlier Than the Male*.

Part of a wrestler's appeal is his fabled lore or backstory. The Mighty Chang was promoted as the Oriental heavy weight champion or the Oriental Hercules and was noted as being able to break three household bricks with one of his dreaded karate chops.[14] Later in 1967 Reid was part of a wrestling tour of India with fellow wrestler Sam Betts—who usually wrestled with an American persona under the name Dwight J. Ingleburgh. As Betts explained, "I knew Milton very well and we were very good friends as we traveled on the road to wrestling events spending time together. I also wrestled him many times. The first time I met Milton was during August of 1967. I was on my way to India and the promoter Don Robinson gave me an extra airline ticket to give to another wrestler who I was to meet at Heathrow airport and that person was Milton Reid. So, we traveled together to India and shared a room while we were there on tour. Shortly after we arrived in India for the tour, Milton went down to visit his sister who owned a hairdresser's shop in Bangalore. It was a real experience in India as malaria was still rampant and you could not drink the water; even the ice was brown from the water.

"In Bombay when we arrived, the promoters picked us up at the airport and they took us round to the hotel where we were staying. We passed the Vallabhbhai Patel Stadium where we would be wrestling and there were huge thirty-foot-tall posters of Milton and I outside the stadium along with fellow wrestlers Klondike Bill and Ski Hi Lee. The first night we were all on the bill performing and there were over 50,000 people there. Also on the bill was Dara Singh, the famous Indian wrestler and Bollywood star, who was the hero of the Indian people and had a huge following.

"As a wrestler, Milton was quite notorious. Being a physically imposing figure with his muscles, Milton relied on his strength for matches—he was a clean wrestler but very strong and powerful.

He was a straightforward power wrestler rather than using any special technique. If Milton locked up with you, he could easily hurt you with his strength. In person, Milton was quite the opposite—a fantastic person and a perfect gentleman

Ursula Andress and Milton Reid in the Bond spoof *Casino Royale*

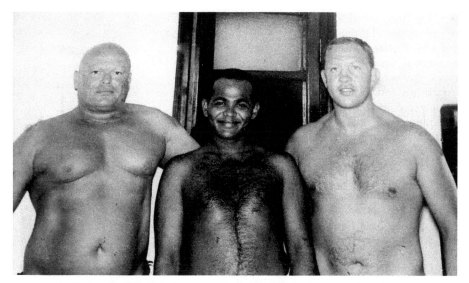

Milton Reid caused a sensation everywhere he went in India.

a rare chance to be involved in an odd-ball musical number called "It Might Be Me"—however Reid and his fellow circus freaks were all lip synching to the song's writer/performer John Scott. Reid would repeat his role as a circus strongman the following year in the concert film *The Rolling Stones Rock and Roll Circus*. Sporting his same look from *Berserk* of a shaved head with a mustache, Reid appeared that year in a thriller called *Target: Harry*. Directed by Roger Corman as a television pilot, *Target: Harry* failed to sell but instead was released two years later in the theaters. The eventual film, starring Vic Morrow as pilot-for-hire Harry Black, was loosely

Milton Reid in *Target: Harry*

in every way. I had seen all of Milton's films previously and especially remember him in *Dr. No*.

"I remember an incident while we were in Bombay, India. Milton had just previously done a film in Rome, and he bought a beautiful suit while there. When the local errand boy came to our room to do the washing Milton asked him if he could dry clean his new suit. The boy quickly said yes, and Milton gave him his suit along with a shirt. Well, I later looked out the back window of the room and I could see Milton's new suit being washed on a rope line. I pointed out the hanging suit to Milton and he got so angry. Now, Milton had not spoken much Indian language during our time on the road together, but when the boy came back, he gave him a round of insults in Hindi! But when the suit came back it was all right.

"Everywhere Milton went in India he caused a sensation. The Indian promoters footed the bill for us wrestlers to eat together, and we used to go out to the most famous hotel in Bombay called the Taj. Milton would show up at the restaurant in this long robe and wearing wooden shoes with big heels on them. He was quite a sight and of course it caused a sensation as soon as everyone recognized him. He usually ordered a large tray of lobsters which he would mostly eat by himself. But he was always fighting over things in the restaurant—nothing seemed to be right for him. I used to think is he doing this for attention. I wasn't happy about this because I knew if you messed with the waiters, they would in return mess your food about. In the back of my mind, I didn't want them spitting in my food.

"The promoter called us up in Bombay to go to Isabod to wrestle. When we got there, they put us in the best hotel

around. We were only there for two days when Milton suddenly left to head to Kashmir where I think he got a job filming there. He brought his wrestling contract with him to the hotel in Kashmir, but the promoter wouldn't pay his new hotel bill. I didn't know anything about this until I got home to England. A week later the manager of the hotel in Bombay sent me a letter asking if I could get in touch with Milton because he did a runner and didn't pay the hotel bill. I did answer the manager back that I didn't know where Milton was then. That was the only bad thing I know about him."[15]

Released the same year as the India wrestling tour, *Berserk* (1967) showcased Reid as a circus strongman and gave him

influenced by the 007 films and featured very similar theme music. In keeping with the theme, the film featured exotic locals, a literally larger-than-life villain played by Victor Buono and his very powerful henchman Kemal played by Reid. Described by his boss as having hands like steel vices, Reid's Kemal is a powerhouse

The cast of *Berserk*: Ted Lune, Golda Casimir, George Claydon, Joan Crawford and Milton Reid

using his deadly hands on the head of a daughter of Black's client. Once again Reid is featured in a wrestling scene, and later, he manhandles Morrow's character knocking him out and throwing him through a table. Like most Bond-type villains Reid's henchman is outwitted when Harry Black batters him with a no crossing signal through a plate glass window which severs his carotid artery. As his boss looks down on the fallen henchman, he quotes Samuel, "And David prevailed over Goliath and smote him and slew him."

With Reid's physical size and intimidating appearance, the idea of him appearing in family theater productions would not immediately spring to mind but he happened to be a perfect fit for a well-known character in literature and folklore—the genie. Reid played a genie often during his career—in theater, television, and film. The first time was in the 1959 West End production of the Cole Porter musical *Aladdin* staged at the Coliseum Theatre in London starring Bob Monkhouse as Aladdin and Doretta Morrow as the princess. The production was based on a CBS television musical from the previous year in which Geoffrey Holder (Baron Samedi from the 1973 James Bond film *Live and Let Die*) had played the genie. So, in both productions there was a 007 connection to the genie character. Reid must have made quite an impression in his performance as the genie since the producers of a 1960 BBC production of *Aladdin* cast him in the same role.

In 1970 Reid returned as the genie in a theater run of *Aladdin* at the London Palladium. Among Reid's cast mates was Sheila Bernette, who shared her memories of him, "Although I hardly bumped into Milton during the production as we were in different scenes, I do remember that he was such a nice and gentle person though a bit shy. The one story I vividly remember involved curtains of all things. During our run of *Aladdin*, we performed two shows every day which was very tiring, and I often fell asleep quickly after returning to my apartment. As my apartment windows were letting in too much light for my liking, I wanted to put up some new curtains. Unfortunately, the wire rope, with a hook on one side and an eye on the other, was rusted and I couldn't take the hook and eye of the rod apart to put new curtains on. I was trying to think of how could I get the rod apart and then thought what if I brought it into the matinee and let the strong man playing the genie pull it apart? So, I brought the rod with me the next day to Milton's dressing room and asked if he could help me. Well Milton kindly offered to help and tried and tried but even he could not get the curtain rod apart with all his strength. That night when I got home, I took one of my books out on cleaning and did a little research on rust—apparently putting the rusted item in a saucer filled with vinegar would be the solution to my problem. The next morning, I took out the hook and eye from the vinegar solution and they came apart immediately. I was so proud that I got them apart that I couldn't wait to get to the matinee and show Milton. When I showed him that I got the hook and eye apart, he was absolutely amazed and aghast and said he would never live that down!"[16] The same year Reid also played another genie in the Turkish adventure film *The Nameless Knight*. Thanks to the special effects done in London, Reid's genie emerges from the bottle and grows to enormous proportions, helping the young hero who sets him free. Similar to his kind genie, Reid often was willing to help those around him and lent his physical strength for a charity fundraiser in 1970 to help support the Acton Blind Social Club.[17]

One of Reid's more memorable death scenes occurred in the 1971 cult classic *Dr. Phibes Rises Again*. Playing a manservant to Robert Quarry's eternal life-seeking explorer Biderbeck, Reid's character is charged with guarding a sacred Egyptian scroll. This sets Reid's

Milton Reid is featured on this Turkish poster for *The Nameless Knight*.

The 1970 *Aladdin* at the London Palladium, features Leslie Crowther, Cilla Black, Sheila Bernette with Milton Reid and Alfred Marks at the back

Reid meets a gruesome death when a dummy phone shoots a deadly spike through his head, in *Dr. Phibes Rises Again*.

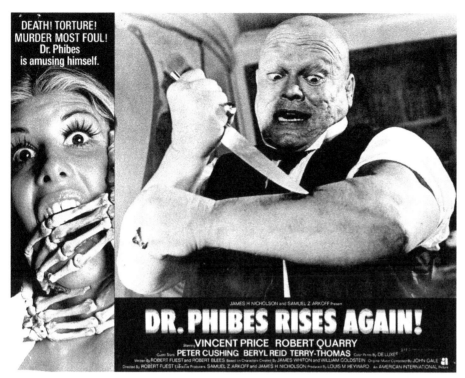

DEATH! TORTURE!
MURDER MOST FOUL!
Dr. Phibes
is amusing himself.

JAMES H NICHOLSON and SAMUEL Z ARKOFF Present

DR. PHIBES RISES AGAIN!

Starring VINCENT PRICE ROBERT QUARRY

Guest Stars PETER CUSHING BERYL REID TERRY-THOMAS Color Prints By DE LUXE®

Written By ROBERT FUEST and ROBERT BLEES Based on Characters Created By JAMES WHITON and WILLIAM GOLDSTEIN Original Music Composed By JOHN GALE
Directed By ROBERT FUEST Executive Producers SAMUEL Z ARKOFF and JAMES H NICHOLSON Produced By LOUIS M HEYWARD An AMERICAN INTERNATIONAL Picture

character in mortal danger as he is targeted by the original owner of the scroll, the genius mastermind Dr. Phibes, played by Vincent Price. Reid's manservant settles down for the night with a well-deserved ale and begins a game of billiards which is suddenly interrupted by venomous snakes (both mechanical and real) unleashed by Phibes. (Pythons standing in for presumably cobras). The scene is quite suspenseful, with Reid reacting to the snakes hissing with a mixture of surprise and bravery. Phibes is a master of trickery, however, and manages to get the best of the manservant. After being lured by a false sense of security and bitten by poisonous fangs, Reid's manservant correctly applies lifesaving measures before running to phone his boss, proving he was not mute for a change even though he had no spoken lines. However, Dr. Phibes' trickery works once again as a dummy phone shoots a spike right through the head of the shocked manservant. The bulging eyes and dead stare on Reid's face is paused for a moment to highlight his unique death. For a non-speaking role, Reid manages to illicit a good amount of sympathy for his character.

In 1973 Reid was involved in his last major wrestling tour which took place in Singapore and Malaysia. As explained by Reid's agent Maurice Aza, "He hardly ever does any wrestling these days. When he does, it's just to fill in the time."[18] Most likely Reid took on his last wrestling tour as a way out of his dire financial position. In late 1972, Reid, listed as a film extra, filed a bankruptcy position as noted in *The Stage*.[19] In Singapore the wrestling tour was booked at Gay World Stadium. As the Mighty Chang, now promoted as from Mongolia, Chang wrestled Bruno Bekkar and Donald Leow in special 30-minute time limit matches during consecutive months.

Wrestler Sam Betts, who also was on the tour, shared his memories, "The last time I was with Milton was during the Southeast Asia tour. He was older and feeling the effects of age—always looking to sleep. He would be sitting and drop off to sleep. I took a photo of him nodding off in a chair in the garden at the hotel in Malaysia, which I liked very much.

"As the Mighty Chang, Milton was an enigmatic who's cultured presence was felt and attracted vast crowds wherever he went. I'll always remember that Milton really enjoyed life. When Milton earned money from wrestling or filming, he would take his wife in his big American car, and they would drive through Europe touring. Their favorite place to visit was Marrakesh in Morocco. He just loved to travel and enjoy his food and drink, but you never saw him smoking or anything like that."[20]

Come Play with Me (1977) marked an unusual turn of events in Reid's life. The softcore sex film starred Mary Millington and was produced and directed by George Harrison Marks. Reid had previously appeared in the sex comedy *Au Pair Girls* (1972) for director Val Guest, but what made his role as a stereotypical thug in *Come Play with Me* different was it was the beginning of Reid's friendship with

star Mary Millington and a working relationship with Marks—which would prove to be his undoing. The film, while nothing to write home about, broke records for playing four years straight at the same cinema. While shooting his scenes on *Come Play with Me*, Reid and Millington became close friends, and afterwards were often seen about town and attending events together. Most notable was the West End premiere of *The Spy Who Loved Me*, in which Reid and Millington were photographed together for the press. This casts some mystery on Reid, as he was married and had children while traveling and posing with a well-known pornographic actress. Unfortunately for Reid, he forgot to bring along his VIP tickets to *The Spy Who Loved Me* premiere and was not allowed in for the screening with his guest. Reid's relationship with Millington also got him in with George Harrison Marks—a British

Reid and wrestler Sam Betts

Reid and Millington at a premiere

glamour photographer who started filming pornographic films on 8mm.

Another example of the sex comedies that Reid appeared in was *Adventures of a Private Eye* (1977), in which he played a bodyguard for a stereotypical Italian gangster named Legs Luigi. Reid's character spent his screen time chasing around the titled private eye. Michael Armstrong, producer and writer of the film, shared his memories of Reid: "My recollections of him are remote, as he was only with us for a few days. Shooting those low-budget schedules, people have little time really to get to know each other. I remember him courting eccentricity by wearing a cloak, carrying an ornate cane, continually citing a spiritual awareness of life and having a young boy in tow following him around like a little lapdog satisfying his every need. Despite this image of grandeur, he was extremely affable if somewhat self-opinionated and couldn't understand why he wasn't cast in leading roles. He asked me if I would be interested in writing a starring role for him that would show everyone that he could handle a dramatic part. He had an idea about the kind of character he wanted to play. I suspect this flattering request had also been made to many, many other writers encountered in his travels. I declined his offer, explaining that I was already heavily committed to other projects for at least the next two years.

"My most vivid memory of Milton was when Stanley took us all out for lunch to a highly-recommended Chinese restaurant near one of the locations. The food, which looked delicious, had no sooner been set down before us when Milton ordered a bottle of tomato ketchup and completely smothered his entire meal with it. The sight of a heaped plateful of beautiful Chinese food covered in tomato ketchup proved sufficient enough to put most of us off our lunch." [21]

After appearing in two sex comedies back-to-back, Reid returned to the world of fantasy in the first of two films for director Kevin Connor. The film, *The People that Time Forgot*, was a sequel to *The Land that Time Forgot* and based upon the stories by Edgar Rice Burroughs. Reid got the choice role as lead villain in the film playing Sabbala, a ruthless primitive leader of the samurai-resembling Nargas. In the hidden prehistoric Antarctic land of Caprona, Sabbala has captured Bower Tyler, played by Doug McClure, whom he keeps as his prisoner. A rescue team organized by Tyler's friend comes to Caprona in hopes of finding the lost explorer and is assisted by a native cavegirl named Ajor, played by Dana Gillespie. After battling dinosaurs along the way, the rescue team reaches the volcano-worshiping Nargas on the Mountain of Skulls where a climactic battle with Sabbala occurs before a massive volcanic explosion. In both films that Reid appeared for Connor he was made up with heavy makeup for his character. As Sabbala, Reid's makeup

makes him look like a cross between a caveman and an overweight Incredible Hulk, sporting green body paint, bushy eyebrows and a massive fur cape and gold chain. Dana Gillespie, who shared scenes with Reid, remembered their time on set, "I can't really say too much about Milton as we only really had one scene together where he had to try to strangle me. Milton was acting so well he managed to nearly do that, as I was choking a bit. We also had to deal with the so-called exploding volcano which was a bit of a challenge thanks to the pyrotechnics crew."[22]

Reid's last role in an official James Bond film took place in *The Spy Who Loved Me* (1977). For Reid, the film had two connections to the 1959 film *Ferry to Hong Kong*. Lewis Gilbert directed both films and Curd Jürgens (now credited with his actual German name spelling) plays the hero in the former film and now the villain in the latter. As Sandor, the henchman for shipping tycoon and evil scientist Karl Stromberg played by Jürgens, Reid had a larger role than his last appearance in the Bond series. In an interview with *Screen International*, Reid was obviously happy with his newest 007 role, "It is an even better part than that of Oddjob in *Goldfinger*. I nearly got to play Oddjob, but Harold Sakata just beat me to it. Now in *The Spy Who Loved Me* I make up for losing Oddjob. Indeed, it is a much more spectacular role. We had a great time shooting these sequences. As Roger has a marvelous sense of humor, and he is a tough and virile man anyway, I really had to go some

Publicity shots taken for *The Spy Who Loved Me*

Roger Moore battles Milton Reid atop a building in *The Spy Who Loved Me*.

to knock him about. He weaved about the set, avoiding my punches like a white Muhammad Ali!"[23]

The film deviated from the Ian Fleming's source novel in all but the title, however Reid's film persona was based on the novel's character Sluggsy Morant, who was described as having a bald head. In the film, Sandor is a thorn in Bond's side (played by Roger Moore) and their inevitable battle happens on a rooftop following Sandor's assassination of a woman in Bond's arms. After chasing Sandor up a flight of stairs onto the roof, Bond is attacked by Sandor who gains a momentary upper hand by putting him in a bear hug, followed by a double judo chop. Bond's advanced fighting skills win out however and Sandor, teetering on the edge of the building by holding his enemy's tie, gives Bond a clue before Bond sends him to his death below, proclaiming he was a helpful chap. The film provided a fitting ending for Reid in the Bond series. He did practically all the rooftop stunts unlike Moore, whose stunt double Martin Grace he threw around for the more physical bits. This did not stop the stunt coordinator, Bob Simmons, from playing a gag on Reid for his final scene in the fight. As explained by star Roger Moore, Reid was

informed by Bob Simmons that he would have to fall off the roof to which Reid complained that it was a six-story drop. Simmons continued to play along saying he could pile up boxes to the fourth story so Reid would only fall for two stories. A desperate Reid tried to reason for a one story drop and a long scream.[24] Reid quickly followed up his last 007 film with an over-the-top spoof on the series, *No. 1 of the Secret Service*, in which he played Eye Patch.

In what was surely a miscarriage of justice, Reid's only acting role playing an actual wrestler involved him not wrestling at all. In the 1978 Leonard Rossiter starring wrestling comedy series, *The Losers*, Reid appeared as the dreaded wrestler The Thing from Catford in the episode of the same name. Announced in the ring, Reid appears in his wrestling trunks and sports a bevy of tattoos, but when it comes time for the match, his opponent, wrapped all in bandages, falls flat on the mat much to his confusion. An odd note occurred in the credits for Reid's episode of *The Losers* as he was listed as Milton Gaylord Reid. His middle name from birth was Rutherford, and that middle name was even once credited in his 1960 television movie of *Aladdin*. He also appeared in another Aladdin film in 1961, *The Wonders of Aladdin* directed by Mario Bava

and starring Donald O'Connor. However, in at least three later television productions, Reid was credited with the middle name Gaylord, and he was credited with that new middle name in the Spotlight actors guide. In fact, his autographs for fans during this time period included the middle name Gaylord as well. He never mentioned in any interviews the reason for the change.

Reid's previous film performances helped him get a role in Norman J. Warren's 1978 horror film *Terror*. As the director recalled, "I didn't spend much time with Milton as I only directed him for

Donald O'Connor and Milton Reid in the Mario Bava film *The Wonders of Aladdin*

LIFE magazine names its ugliest models, and Milton Reid is included.

one day on *Terror*. I was so pleased that we were able to hire him even though it was for a tiny part as the bouncer in the club because he seemed to be a part of my teenage years. What I mean is that I seemed to grow up watching him at the cinema, as he was in so many films. For me Milton was quite a celebrity, and it was just good to have him around. It was a joy meeting him. The one thing that was surprising was that he was such a gentle man. He was both a very gentle person and had a very gentle voice. He never seemed to speak in many of his films. I was under the impression that his voice would go along with that very strong and intimidating body that he had. But his voice was actually very quiet and gentle, the opposite of what you would imagine. He was just a very nice guy all around.

"He was very worried when I spoke to him about doing the film because he was suffering a condition known as muscle bound. This was due to all his wrestling and bodybuilding he did when he was younger. The condition occurs due to overdeveloping your muscles; when you get older the muscles cannot go back to the way they were, so they become very weak as a result. Milton explained to me that he could no longer run, so for his role as the bouncer taking out the rowdy customer, he could only walk over to him and walk him out. It didn't matter for his role, however. He also couldn't move his arms around too quickly for the same reason. I knew what he meant as I had a friend who many years ago did weightlifting to build up his muscles and over time could no longer put his finger and thumb together anymore. So, Reid unfortunately paid the price for his large size.

"Not only was Milton a part of my childhood growing up and watching him in the cinemas, but I also lived not very far away from him. He lived in a place called Shepherd's Bush, and I was living about two miles away in Hammersmith. I would always see him driving about in a Ford Galaxy or Chevrolet—a bright red '60s convertible in which he always had the top down no matter what the weather was. He would cruise around town with the sunglasses he wore in *Terror*. He was just a familiar sight and quite a showstopper because everyone would look at him due to the combination of the bright red car with the top down and his massive size. Even if it was raining, he would still have the top down. I'm pretty sure he loved the attention he would get being recognized on the street. It probably dates to him being a wrestler, as that was all show business anyway, and being in films was just a continuation of the two. You couldn't miss him on the street, he wasn't a very tall man, but his shoulders were very broad.

"He was very easy to work with, a gentle and nice guy all around. He would do whatever he could to please you as a director. Sadly, we didn't have more for him to do but it was still nice to have him in the film and on set. I like when I can do that because the nice thing about films is that you can capture the person forever and they will never change in the film. Fortunately, because we were making our own film, we didn't have to go to a producer for permission—we could choose whoever we wanted to use. Another sad thing about Milton was that when we filmed *Terror*, he was over 60 years old and still living in Shepherd's Bush in this small house. Even sadder was that this wonderful car of his that I remembered from years previous was sitting outside and rusting away from exposure to the weather. The reason it was just sitting there as Milton explained was that the transmission had gone out and he could never afford to have it fixed. So, it just sat there and rotted away.

"I found out about Milton's car because I wound up picking up Milton on the morning to bring him to the set as we lived so close together and so we had a nice opportunity to chat in the car before we had to start work. I had heard rumors that he had that same issue previously a few times not being able to pay his bills. This was most likely due to his short roles and mostly non-speaking parts. I mean if you don't speak in the movies, especially in those days with the union, you just didn't get paid the higher amounts. In England certainly that was the heyday of the unions which completely controlled the industry. So, he wouldn't have been a big earner and he certainly did seem to quite enjoy his life a lot when he was younger. He most likely was not thinking much about the future which is true of all of us when we were younger. It was a sad time in his life, and he wasn't working much from what he was saying to me and that's why he enjoyed coming to spend the day with us and be around a film crew again. It wasn't long after that that he disappeared."[25]

In *Arabian Adventure*, Reid would play the genie once more and would go out with a bang. His genie emerged from a bottle in a mist of smoke thanks to the special effects and had the unique look of studded metal bands, a blue head and

Milton Reid in *Arabian Adventure*

Milton Reid with hair!

bulging eyes due to a set of prosthetic eyes. Unlike the traditional genie, Reid's character isn't exactly grateful to the people who let him out of the bottle, happily telling them he will kill them and will grant them one favor—a quick and merciful death. True to his word, Reid's genie proceeds to shoot lightning bolts from his hands at his saviors. Just when it seems like the hero is doomed, the hero grabs the genie's bottle forcing him to give up and become a humble slave. It's too late though as even though he gives the hero the information to continue their quest, the hero's assistant tosses the bottle into a mountain, transforming the genie into a stone monument.

The film's director, Kevin Connor, remembers working with Reid, "I directed Milton in two films—*The People that Time Forgot* and *Arabian Adventure*. In the second film he played the genie in the bottle which entailed just a day's work. He was very placid, gentle and quiet. He asked what he had to do, and we re-voiced him (with Valentine Dyall). It was a small role which seemed to be mostly what he got during his career. The casting director recommended Milton on both occasions. I directed him as he had such a great look for those types of movies. He came from the East End of London and had a very modest background. He was very professional and did his job splendidly—not just going through the motions. Unfortunately, it was a small role, so he came and went. As with most British actors the role is just a job and they do it professionally and with a lot of grace. I held onto the sword that Milton used in *People the World Forgot* and my son has it now.[26]

Despite appearing in films and well-known to the public, Reid admitted in court that he was essentially living off £20

a week from social security when he was brought in for a £40 fine for reckless driving and not having a driving license.[27] It was perhaps this situation that led to Reid making bad decisions to earn some additional money. While Reid had appeared in three other sexploitation films with his friend Mary Millington—*What's Up Superdoc!* and *Confessions from the David Galaxy Affair* and *Queen of the Blues*, his additional films for director/producer George Harrison Marks arguably marked the end of his film career in England. In 1979 Reid appeared in three 8mm porn films for Marks which included non-sexual cameos in two hardcore films and a more hands on role in the softcore film *Bustman's Holiday*. The *Sunday People* magazine apparently were tipped off on the making of the films and ran a piece on them, exposing Reid's involvement. The result was a loss of work for the actor. In a letter to writer/director Simon Sheridan, Reid stated that, "I was harmed as I did a lot of charity work."[28] In addition, Reid's friend Mary Millington, who had battled with depression and run-ins with the law for years, took her own life the same year. With Reid outed for his appearance in the hardcore loops, his advertising gigs dried up. Besides his most well-known spot playing a bodyguard in the Ogdens St. Bruno's tobacco rough cut television commercials, Reid also advertised for Chelsea Cloister's garage Eagle exhaust service, Kemital Plastics and a tire company with the brilliant slogan featuring Reid's head and stating tires should have treads on them, not be bald. Trying to capitalize on his look, Reid became one of the first actors represented by a new agency in Shepherd's Bush called Ugly Enterprises.[29] Reid chimed in on his own appearance, "I don't think I'm ugly. But then, I'm behind it all, so I can't really tell."[30]

Reid's very last appearance in a U.K. production was playing the title beast in an episode of the BBC2 anthology television series, *West Country Tales* episode "The Beast." Although he had no lines as usual, Reid's appearance as the beast was truly frightening, sporting nothing much more than pointy teeth and dirty makeup. With his wrestling career over and acting jobs drying up quickly in England, Reid decided to go back to his native country and try his luck in Bollywood. In addition, Reid's mother and sister still lived in the city of Bangalore. A month after arriving, Reid found himself in trouble with the law

One of many agency cards Milton possessed

again while trying to assist his family. As reported by the *Times of India*, Reid was arrested on charges of trespassing, damaging furniture and disconnecting a telephone after tenants of his sister's sprawling Grant Road bungalow complained that he was harassing them. Most likely Reid was trying to evict non-paying tenants to help his sister which spiraled out of control. Police noted the 64-year-old Reid became abusive and violent when they tried to arrest him. He was eventually remanded to judicial custody pending a court date.[31]

Reid's luck with Bollywood didn't fare well either. He only made three films before seemingly disappearing altogether. In his very last film, *Kala Dhanda Goray Log* (1986), Reid got to play an over-the-top villainous ruler in an extravagant palace. Wearing blue eye liner, gold shorts and a white fur vest, Reid projected a striking figure. With plenty of guards and an overly excited midget court jester, Reid's boss character delights in grossing out his advisors by eating live frogs. A customary Bollywood dance number ensues during which Reid's ruler is slipped a frog con-

Reid in *West Country Tales* **episode "The Beast"**

Peter Wyngarde and Milton Reid on the set of the television series *Department 5.*

15. Interview with Sam Betts by the author, 2019

16. Interview with Sheila Bernette by the author, 2019

17. "Four Strong Men and a Great Success," *Acton Gazette* April 30, 1970

18. "Milton Makes it Big," *Gazette and Post* January 14, 1971

19. *The Stage*, Aug 9, 1973

20. Interview with Sam Betts by the author, 2019

21. Interview with Michael Armstrong by the author, 2019

22. Interview with Dana Gillespie by the author, 2019

23. Interview with Milton Reid, *Screen International*

24. *My Word Is My Bond: A Memoir; Bond On Bond; and Last Man Standing: Tales From Tinseltown* by Sir Roger Moore

25. Interview with Norman J. Warren by the author, 2019

26. Interview with Kevin Connor by the author, 2019

27. "Milton Reid—Muscle Man of the Films," *Hammersmith & Shepherds Bush Gazette* March 23, 1978.

28. "Milton and Mary—The Odd Couple" by Simon Sheridan, 2012.

29. "How They Face up to a Fortune," *Daily Mirror* May 24, 1979

30. "Milton Makes it Big," *Gazette and Post* January 14, 1971

31. "Actor of Bond Film Arrested in India," *The Straits Times* Aug 5, 1981

*Special thanks to Steve Ogilvie for the Mighty Chang photos

taining explosives and meets his end when it is detonated. Certainly, an over-the-top ending for an over-the-top character. Reid himself disappeared from the public shortly after making the film and even his son stopped receiving letters which most likely points to the wrestler/actor passing away sometime in 1987. A somewhat sad end for the mighty Milton Reid, but he surely lived life to the fullest and left an impact that will not be forgotten in both wrestling and film.

FOOTNOTES

1. IMDb

2. Interview with Sam Betts by the author, 2019

3. www.forces-war-records.co.uk

4. "Why Mr. Woo Feels Blue," *The Advertiser* January 22, 1959

5. Interview with Sam Betts by the author, 2019

6. Wrestlingheritage.co.uk

7. "How They Face up to a [For]tune," *Daily Mirror* May 24, 1979

8. "Why Mr. Woo Feels Blue," *Advertiser* January 22, 1959

9. "A Curt 'No'?" *Daily Mirror* 6, 1959

10. Interview with Michael C[ox]ford by the author courtesy of Knight/Knight Ayton Managem[ent] 2020

11. Interview with Johnny Ki[?] by the author, 2020

12. "Wrestlers Grapple Over P[?] Film," *Daily Mirror* Jan 3, 1964

13. "Dr. No Strong Man Had [?] Trouble in Rome," *Hammersmith & [Shep]herd's Bush Gazette* Dec 9, 1965

14. "Wrestling at Glastonbury T[own] Hall, Cheddar Valley Gazette," No[v] 1967

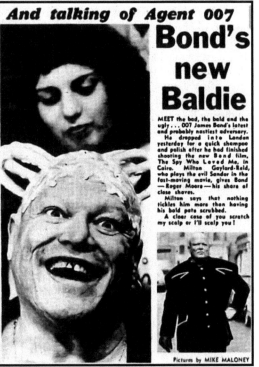

And talking of Agent 007

Bond's new Baldie

MEET the bad, the bald and the ugly... 007 James Bond's latest and probably nastiest adversary. He dropped into London yesterday for a quick shampoo and polish after he had finished shooting the new Bond film, The Spy Who Loved Me, in Cairo. Milton Gaylord-Reid, who plays the evil Sandor in the fast-moving movie, gives Bond — Roger Moore—his share of close shaves.

Milton says that nothing tickles him more than having his bald pate scrubbed.

A clear case of you scratch my scalp or I'll scalp you!

Pictures by MIKE MALONEY

AIDAN QUINN   KATE BECKINSALE   ANTHONY ANDREWS   JOHN GIELGUD

A CRITICAL APPRECIATION
BY BARRY ATKINSON

HAUNTED

Lewis Gilbert's adaptation of James Herbert's 1988 novel *Haunted* is one of the most exquisite of all ghost films to have been produced over the past 25 years, yet it remains largely undiscovered. [Contains Spoilers] Shot on a decent budget of just under £1,000,000, the 15-rated movie (suitable for 15-year-olds in the UK) was released by Lumière Films in October 1995 and was a moderate box-office success. To his credit, veteran director Gilbert, who had been at the helm of some of Britain's biggest box-office smashes (three *James Bond* outings plus *Reach for the Sky*, *Sink the Bismark!*, *Alfie*, *Educating Rita* and *Shirley Valentine*), and with the help of scriptwriters Timothy Prager and Bob

Kellett, eschewed a lot of Herbert's sometimes rambling prose and made significant alterations to the narrative, thus presenting a streamlined version of perhaps one of the author's shortest books; many critics have found Herbert's novels to be on the lengthy side, with too much emphasis on the roll-call of horrors and padded out with too many peripheral characters and superfluous dialogue, but not this one ("Little finesse … all crude power," Stephen King once quoted of Herbert's style). What we are presented with is a finely wrought and pretty-creepy tale of guilt and supernatural revenge dressed up in Tony Pierce-Robert's glossy Technicolor hues, old-fashioned in conception,

where modern-day jump-scare tactics are thankfully noticeable by their absence here; they're not needed, the goosebumps created by a sense of unreality allied to a cold malevolence from beyond the grave.

It's the year 1928: American Professor David Ash (Aidan Quinn), working in the field of parapsychology, is a firm disbeliever in the spirit world, having spent his entire adult life debunking the existence of ghosts. As a child in Sussex, 1905, he was playing with his twin sister Juliet (Victoria Shalet) on the banks of a lake when he accidently pushed her, causing her to topple off a bridge crossing a stream; she struck her head, rolled into the waters and drowned (the movie opens with this sequence); diving in to save her, he saw her body slowly drift away into a diffused tunnel of light among the dense green weeds. Later, he stole downstairs to the sound of her voice coming from far off. Approaching her coffin in a sweat, he planted a kiss on her forehead; her eyes opened, and she mouthed, "Uh," an eerie scene that unsettles the nerves—and there are plenty more similar moments to follow! Still wracked with guilt over her death, he has written a book on the paranormal and lectures his students at Camberley University, instructing them to adopt a scientific approach when studying such phenomena. "If you want my opinion, there are no ghosts … there is only the longing that there should be to ease our pain and our fears."

Next, we see the Professor exposing a medium during a séance, but is she as fake as he reckons her to be? The woman at one point mentions "Ed Brook? Edward Brook? Edbrook?" and as David exits the room, labeling the medium "a despicable fraud," he hears, or *thinks* he hears, Juliet's voice whispering, "David. Please. Please." Back at his office, his secretary, Kate (Geraldine Somerville), informs him that another letter has been received from a Miss Webb at Edbrook Hall, pleading for his help; she claims to be tormented by evil spirits and is becoming desperate. David recalls the medium's words, "Ed Brook? Edbrook?" and, both puzzled and intrigued, decides to investigate the case, boarding the train to Edbrook and met on the station by Christina Mariell, who emerges like an apparition out of the billowing engine steam; 22-year-old Kate Beckinsale plays her, a bewitching vision of English Rose-loveliness, even though her pallor is deathly white, offset by a pair of ruby-red lips. In her top-of-the-range Wolseley automobile, they speed through the countryside, drawing up at the imposing Edbrook Hall (Parham House in Par-

Christina Mariell (Kate Beckinsale) emerges like an apparition out of the billowing engine steam.

ham Park near Storrington, West Sussex, was used for location filming, six miles down the road from where I once lived). Entering the house, Miss Tess Webb (Anna Massey) nervously greets them, the children's nanny looking distinctly shaky and anguished. "It's this ghost business," explains Christina. "She's obsessed with it." David is shown to his room, white dust sheets covering most of the furnishings, a semi-nude portrait of Christina adorning one wall. He's then introduced to Robert Mariell (Anthony Andrews, the movie's co-producer) who admits giving Nanny Tess a copy of his book which "started all this nonsense and you coming down here." Robert, amiable enough at first, is surrounded by numerous paintings of Christina displaying her ample breasts; in fact, he's busy working on another similar portrait. All very odd, muses David, who wonders whether the supposed hauntings could be the work of a local practical joker—perhaps he should have taken more notice of Robert's later comment, made down by the lake: "We're all mad, you know."

At the lakeside, Christina strips off (a body double was used for Beckinsale's nude shots), David watching, his piercing blue eyes on stalks; briefly, Juliet, David's sister, is glimpsed floating among the weeds. Then "the joker in the pack" arrives, Simon (Alex Lowe), Christina's second brother, who takes off his clothes

and joins his sister. "Admiring our pet mermaid? Quite stunning, isn't she?" grins Robert who has turned up, brother and sister clambering out of the lake and running off towards the house. "Yes,

she is," agrees David. In the night, David has a nightmarish dream about pallbearers carrying a coffin outside in the mist. Waking, he detects a scratching at the door, followed by a loud banging. The

A montage of photos from *Haunted* (1995)

door seems to be locked but, opening it, the corridor is empty, the house strangely still and unnaturally quiet. At breakfast the next morning, Christina opines that the door-locking incident must be attributed to "Nanny's ghost," David later noticing Miss Webb talking to herself, or to someone, in the kitchen, again appearing detracted and agitated, as if pestered by some unseen presence. She tells him that both parents died in India some years ago and he surmises that the woman needs a doctor, not a sceptic like himself.

The three siblings go out for the night to honor a long-standing engagement, but Miss Webb still seems confused, muttering away to herself. "Who were you talking to?" asks David. "Are they still here?" "They'll always be here," moans Nanny. "I thought you came to help me." "I see nothing. The point is, you do," replies the psychic investigator. "There are spirits in this house," Nanny continues before choking, gasping, and running off. "What are you doing? No, no," David hears her frightened voice in the distance as he sets up his forensic equipment to uncover any signs of paranormal activity; there's a flash and Doctor Doyle (John Gielgud) materializes out of the smoke, come to check on Nanny Tess. However, she recoils in terror at the sight of him entering her room, sobbing, "Oh no, no, no." Her door closes to the sound of, "No, no, please, I'll be all right," and then uncontrollable bouts of crying. "Nanny's nerves are shattered," states the doctor afterwards to David. "An emotional trauma … try to persuade her that Edbrook's not haunted."

It's about 36 minutes into the film that those cinemagoers experienced in sitting through umpteen features of the supernatural variety over the years (and

22-year-old Kate Beckinsale shows her deathly pallor and ruby-red lips.

even those who haven't read the book) will probably gather what is going on so, spoiler alert, you can put two and two together and deduce that those three young adults, plus the benign doctor, are in reality the phantoms haunting Edbrook, although blinkered David Ash hasn't yet realized it. And that's the fun to be had from Gilbert's spooky drama: When will the cynic cotton on to the fact that delectable Christine, sinister Robert and prankster Simon are not what they appear to be, and, more importantly, why? The clues are there for all to see: the uncanny silence (Debbie Wiseman's classical-sounding, low-key score is used sparingly to accentuate that silence); that vivid dream; a small girl flit-

ting around the grounds; a door opening on its own; Nanny Tess, seemingly on the verge of a nervous breakdown, being tormented by persons unknown and her alarming reaction in the doctor's presence; Christina's pallor and a piano playing when no one is present (a good old ghost story standby). But David is unable, or unwilling, to accept them as nothing more than normal happenings. At the piano, he goes to kiss Christina, there's a chilly sigh as the atmosphere is disturbed and, just for an instant, a child's legs are seen dangling from the piano stool. In the passage, a gaslight explodes, flames almost engulfing the corridor before mysteriously melting away, the two brothers arriving out of the smoke. "Don't touch the gas," Robert snarls at David, adding pointedly, "I think it's time for bed, Christina, don't you?"

"You were invited into our house to help Nanny. Don't abuse my sister's hospitality, will you," Robert, turning increasingly hostile, levels at David the next day; he's noticed Christina's growing attachment (and lust?) to the academic and for some reason doesn't like it. "I'll finish my work tonight and I'll go tomorrow as planned. Unless of course you want me to leave now," responds David. "No, no," says Robert, who fixes David with an icy stare. "Tomorrow will be adequate."

Another couple of clues for David to grasp occurs when, following a horse ride over the cliffs (East Sussex's Beachy Head) and a romp in a barn, an old fortune tell-

David Ash (Aidan Quinn) and Christina

lake while the balance of her mind was disturbed; she didn't die in India but committed suicide at Edbrook, a fact that Christina admits is true. "I don't trust anyone or anything in this house," David exclaims; maybe now, his non-belief in the supernatural is beginning to crumble just a tad.

Outside, in the dark, David thinks he sees Juliet's small figure among the trees and stops to peer through a lighted window, catching sight of Robert repeatedly kissing Christina as he paints her posing naked. A cellar fire which disperses as soon as it bursts into life ("There's no fire, David.") forces the Professor into visiting the doctor who informs him that he is suffering from emotional stress, just like Nanny Tess, brought on by fighting in the war and grieving over the loss of his twin sister. At the house, David, surprise, suprise, ends up in bed with Christina, Robert observing the copulating pair from the shadows with a mix of jealousy and malice.

In the morning, she's gone. The house is utterly deserted and deathly silent apart from a keening wind. Piles of dead leaves litter the floors and the drapes over the furnishings are now black, not white. No one is about. David then follows his sister's specter through the woods, reaching a nearby church where, among the gravestones, is one proclaiming that the three Mariell children died in "The Great Fire of Edbrook House 1923." The doctor's house is also derelict and abandoned; he's long since passed away, like the Mariells. "Take my hand. Be safe with me," coos Christina, waiting by her car, to a bemused David, Juliet interrupting with, "Don't go to her David." He and Christina drive off ("I'll never leave you, David. We'll be together forever."), much too fast,

er reads David's palm, stating that he will have "a child, one who will be named as the loved one you lost as a child." Grasping Christina's palm, she closes it. "There is nothing I can tell you that you do not know," she utters, her perky mood doused; she quickly leaves with a curt, "Pardon me." She was fully aware that there was something "wrong" about Christina; why can't David acknowledge it.

Back at the mansion, after a brief visit to the summerhouse where an old rocking chair starts to creak of its own accord, Robert shows his annoyance. "Where have you been?" he shouts at the couple. "Out riding? At night? Nanny was worried sick." Returning to the summerhouse, David scatters chalk over the floor; a vortex rises, David following the swirling column down to the lake where a fierce wind forces him into the water, Christina and Robert hauling him out, but not before he has seen Juliet among the weeds ("I didn't fall. I was pushed! A person pushed me!"). Is she trying to warn him of a danger in the house? Drying out in bed with the help of Christina, Robert walks in with a drink to find the pair kissing. "You'll probably need your sleep, Christina," he snaps, glowering at David. After he's left, the door opens and Nanny rushes in, more worried than ever. "I'm not mad, am I, Professor? Take me with you tomorrow. You're my salvation. I beg you!" She's then picked up by an invisible force, both feet lifted clear off the floor, and dragged backwards through the door which slams violently and locks. David smashes open the door and sees Nanny

tucked up in bed, apparently asleep. Yet despite this harrowing occurrence, he still refuses to believe Edbrook Hall is haunted!

In the morning, David, at long last slowly becoming convinced that something peculiar *is* going on, announces to a disappointed Robert that he's not yet ready to leave. Discovering an old newspaper dated February 17, 1923, in a dusty attic, the top half of one page missing, he telephones Kate with orders to carry out a spot of detective work. Downstairs, the siblings, and a distraught-looking Nanny are playing party games in fancy dress, David hiding in a kitchen cupboard and discovered by Christina who kisses him. The missing portion of the paper shows that Mrs. Mariell drowned herself in the

Robert Mariell (Anthony Andrews) in front of a nude portrait of Christina

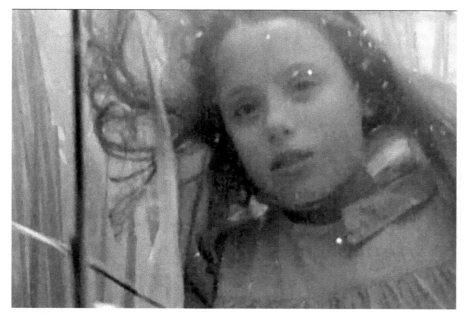

The drowning death of Juliet (Victoria Shalet) is recalled at various points throughout the movie.

the vehicle crashing into a tree when Juliet is spotted standing in the road. The Wolseley erupts into flames, David managing to stagger out, Christina slumped in the driving seat. "Christina's dead!" he howls at Nanny Tess in the hallway but we all knew that, didn't we. "Of course, she is," confirms Nanny. "Forgive me. I should never have asked you here. They'll never let us go." She then reveals to David that the cause of their mother killing herself was because she found Robert and Christina, both intoxicated, in bed together indulging in sex, Simon looking on, and couldn't live with the thought of her children involved in an incestuous relationship. In reprisal, Nanny Tess locked them in their room and set fire to the house, Christina, Robert, and Simon perishing in the inferno.

The three siblings suddenly present themselves, each dressed in black. "It was you," Nanny points to Robert in accusation. "You were born evil." "You locked us in the bedroom. You set fire to it," spits Robert. "They deserved to die," Nanny retaliates. "She killed us, you see," Robert glances at David. "She thought she'd be rid of us." They grab hold of Nanny, spinning her round and round until she expires, leaving David alone with the wraiths. "Face eternity with me." Christina's sepulchral voice seems to come from beyond the grave. "Die for me, David." The Professor tries to leave the burning building, but all the doors are firmly locked and bolted. In the accursed bedroom, the siblings' gloating faces take shape amid the conflagration

and Juliet's small form also manifests itself, holding out her hand for David. He grasps it and the room reverts instantly to its charred state, as hushed as a tomb. Departing from a scorched, blackened Edbrook Hall, Juliet bids a final farewell to her brother, absolving him of all guilt over her drowning, and walks away, disappearing into the afterlife, a quite moving closure between brother and sister. David takes a train back home and alights at the station, Kate there to greet him. "Did you scare all the ghosts away?" she asks. "Most of them," he smiles. As they stroll off the platform, Christina, still dressed in black, follows, her form vanishing into the steam; she's not finished with David yet! (In the book, she boards his carriage

and attacks him, but Gilbert viewed this as one climax too many and dropped it.)

Over the course of 108 minutes, Gilbert's measured pacing, a display of believable acting, an intelligent script, and the brooding Gothic aura that surrounds Edbrook Hall work their magic, ensuring that, with the minimum of effects admirably achieving their aim, this traditional "things that go bump in the night" yarn delivers enough satisfying shivers to appease all fans of the genre. Oh, that today's frenetic, noisy, ghoul-laden offerings could match the expertise, polish and subtlety that make the often overlooked *Haunted* such a vital addition to the sphere of the classic ghost/haunted house film and a real pleasure to sit through.

An intense encounter between Aidan Quinn and Kate Beckinsale.

VILLAGE OF THE DAMNED
LOCATIONS THEN AND NOW

ARTICLE BY RAY AND GAIL ORWIG
PHOTOS COURTESY OF PETER AND ALISON GRAFTON

There are some strange goings-on in the English countryside. Gordon Zellaby (George Sanders) is seen talking to his brother-in-law Alan Bernard (Michael Gwynn) on the phone—and suddenly, he slumps to the ground. Gordon's dog, who was lying nearby, is also motionless. A man driving a tractor has seemingly passed out, and the tractor goes in circles: It runs into a tree and stops. A man with a wheelbarrow, a telephone operator, and a man in his car are shown—all lying still.

Alan Bernard is understandably shaken—the call his brother-in-law Gordon was trying to make was from the town of Midwich.

When outsiders try to approach the varying situations involving fallen residents, they, too, pass out. A caged canary is shown crossing the invisible line, to help mark the perimeter of the area where people have fallen. Strangely, when the bird is pulled back, it revives. Whatever has happened seems to have just affected Midwich. Gas masks are used, in case whatever caused people to pass out en masse is airborne.

And—as quickly as it started—it was over. Approximately four hours later, all the living in the town of Midwich come

to. People complain of feeling chilled but feel otherwise okay. The military comes in and asks questions, testing the inhabitants. People seem to be back to normal … except for one thing.

All women of child-bearing age in Midwich are expecting babies—including women who never had relations with men (which makes for some awkward situations, to say the least). Gordon's wife Anthea (Barbara Shelley) is also expecting. When examined at five months, the fetuses look like the mothers-to-be are in their seventh month. And all 12 babies are born the same day—all with yellow irises.

… and that's not all. As time passes, the 12 children develop at an accelerated rate—four months after they are born, they can do things normally done by a one-and-a-half-year-old. Later, they can control behaviors of those around them and read minds—including each others. If one child learns something, the others already know what the one has learned. As Zellaby takes on the task of educating the 12 children, he finds out from his son David (Martin Stephens) that the strange children are there to learn from him. Zellaby also finds the 12 have the power to kill and are not afraid to demonstrate this power. There were other "children"

born in other countries like these 12, but they didn't survive.

Zellaby must stop the Midwich children.

Village of the Damned was released in 1960, and was based on the John Wyndham novel *The Midwich Cuckoos*. The filming schedule was six weeks in length, and it was shot in Elstree and Letchmore Heath, Radlett, Watford in county Hertfordshire, South East England (conveniently located close by the studio, Borehamwood). About 18 miles from London, one can travel to Hertfordshire via M1, A41 or M25.

To the delight of the movie's fans, many of the sites are still there. Some of the filming locations you can visit:

Barbara Shelley signing autographs at FANEX 15 in Baltimore, Maryland

(left) The Zellaby Estate, then known as Aldenham House. (right) Now the Haberdashers' Aske's Boys' School off Aldenham Road in Elstree, located in Hertfordshire. This view can be seen from a distance from Aldenham Road. The school grounds are closed to the public.

(left) Church of St. John the Baptist in Aldenham, Hertfordshire. (right) Same building, minus the clock! (The clock was placed on the church wall for filming. The locals did not like it and had it removed.) Located on Church Lane, Radlett, Watford.

(left) The Green in Letchmore Heath, located between The Green and Back Lane. (right) The War Memorial can be seen on the left in both shots. Located at Radlett, Watford.

(left) Doctor Willers (Laurence Naismith) leaves 2 and 3 Landor Cottages on Back Lane, Letchmore Heath, Radlett, Watford. (right) Those cottages looking nearly the same today. (If you visit Letchmore Heath, please respect the privacy of the occupants—thank you!)

(left) Three Horseshoes Pub, located at The Green, Letchmore Heath, Radlett, Watford. (right) How it appears today.

The village stores located at 3, Back Lane, Letchmore Heath, Radlett, Watford. (right) A contemporary view of the same site.

(left) The famous wall, at the end of Back Lane, Letchmore Heath, Radlett, Watford. (right) The film makes it look like a dead-end road, but it is actually an intersection of Back Lane and Common Lane.

(left) Three Horseshoes Pub, located at The Green, Letchmore Heath, Radlett, Watford. (right) How it appears today.

Notes:

Just to let the readers know, there are many pubs with the same name (Three Horseshoes) in England.

The limestone cross War Memorial on the village green was erected in 1920. It is a combined War Memorial, listing the 55 known soldiers who perished in both WWI and WWII.

Martin Stephens (who played David Zellaby) studied architecture as an adult. London-born Barbara Shelley, who played Anthea Zellaby in *Village of the Damned*, was a science fiction fan. Miss Shelley had fond memories of reading science fiction-related magazines with her dad growing up. When she was offered roles in science fiction film, she was already open to ideas of the fantastic. Barbara Shelley was also a FANEX Convention guest. We lost Miss Shelley to COVID-19, January 3, 2021. This article is dedicated to Barbara Shelley.

Sources:

Internet Movie Database: location information https://www.imdb.com/title/ tt0054443/locations?ref_=tt_ql_dt_5 Reelstreets https://www.reelstreets.com/films/village-of-the-damned/ There are 44 screenshots on this site for *Village of the Damned*!)

HORROR STRIKES THE FAMILIAR
... WHEN YOU LEAST EXPECT IT!
BY GARY J. SVEHLA

Many observe outright love of the films made during the 1950s in the horror and science fiction genres. Consider alien invaders, giant insect pictures, monsters from space, robots, modern vampires and werewolves (even decendents of Dr. Frankenstein were trying to replicate human life), mutant life forms. etc. Films such as *The Thing, Invaders from Mars, I Was a Teenage Werewolf* and *Frankenstein, The Vampire, The Werewolf, 20 Million Miles to Earth, Invasion of the Body Snatchers, Earth vs. the Giant Spider, Horror of Dracula*, and *The Monster That Challenged the World* filled our adolescent minds with a sense of wonder.

These films may not be revered as much as horror classics of the 1930s, but they were popular and film critics were bound to have fun with them, often using hyperbole and playing up the non-sensible nature that most of them held.

But I have a theory why they grew in popularity over the decades. These films at the time were appreciated, but the popularity of horror and science fiction films of the 1950s grew exponentially in the following decades. People realized this cinematic fare may not be as good as the classic monsters of old, but these films are more endearing, warm and fuzzy. And let me explain why.

Nostalgia! The familiar.

When you lived in the era when children on bikes delivered prescriptions from neighborhood drug stores or doctors made house calls when you had the flu was ordinary. But when you moved a few decades further beyond this more-gentle reality and realized you had to see the doctor, not the other way around, doctors making house calls suddenly became nostalgic. Thoughts of a kinder world where kids could play on neighborhood streets without being molested, kidnapped or shot became endearingly thought of as the good old days where you knew and trusted your neighbors. This type of world becomes like a warm hug, even while it was moving further and further into your past and becoming more distant. These cuddly moments from decades ago were encased in feelings of warmth and safety.

But such insulating remembrances from the past soon became populated with monsters and horrors that invaded our psyche, destroying our sense of the familiar and the safety of our childhood. Suddenly modern horrors infringed upon our care-

John Beal as the sympathic vampire, staring at a cage of vampire bats.

In a studio publicity shot, John Beal carries the defenseless Coleen Gray.

free daydreams which quickly transformed into nightmares and threatened to invade our glory days of security. Even if the horrors of the present were unavoidable, our sweet past was threatened.

So let me take you through six iconic 1950s films, some science fiction, some horror, that illustrate this sense of the familiar and show why genre 1950s films take on an ever-increasing popularity of their own.

First let us consider United Artists' 1957 release, *The Vampire*, starring John Beal, Kenneth Tobey and Coleen Gray. In this sequence it is nighttime in small-town America. Coleen Gray is cautiously walking down a neighborhood street, her face registers fear that something is following her. She nervously looks back but sees

nothing threatening her (take our her). But once she turns and glances backward at the bright streetlight a second time, she sees a silhouetted shadow of a man or fiend following her, dodging behind trees and then running at breakneck speed toward her. She utters a quiet "oohoo" be-

fore running faster down the silent suburban street, passing a multitude of quaint picket fences and front lawns as she heads for the safety of her home, which she finally reaches. Fumbling for her keys and making it inside, she locks the front door but sees the lock twist back and forth as

A Mexican lobby card for *The Vampire*, the scene depicted shows a father's love for his daughter.

John Beal sits at his office desk trying to figure out what's gone wrong.

EDWARD L. ALPERSON
presents

INVADERS FROM MARS

PHOTOGRAPHED IN
COLOR

HELENA CARTER · ARTHUR FRANZ · JIMMY HUNT

AN EDWARD L. ALPERSON PRODUCTION

WILLIAM CAMERON MENZIES · RICHARD BLAKE

EDWARD L. ALPERSON, JR. · RAOUL KRAUSHAAR 20.

someone tries to get inside. Suddenly the fiend stops the attempt, and Coleen Gray leans against the safety of her wall as she collapses and starts to sob.

Meanwhile, out on the street, an old lady is walking her pet dog, telling her dog not to tire out, since their home is right around the corner. Mrs. Dietz pulls her little dog along, as the animal starts to turn and bark. Priscilla, her dog, now frantically barks, Mrs. Dietz telling the pet to quiet down, so she will not wake up the neighborhood. Then, suddenly, from out of the darkness, the vampire leaps for Mrs. Dietz, knocking her to the ground as Priscilla runs for cover in the brush of a nearby yard, whimpering as

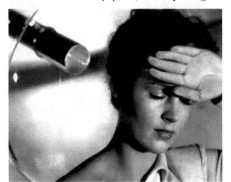

The underground Martian colony where humans are injected with mind-controlling transmitters and released to do their bidding.

her mistress is strangled lying defenseless on the sidewalk. Soon, neighbors rush outside to examine Mrs. Dietz, who is beyond help, as her dog runs to be by her side.

Today, one might be very cautious to walk alone under cover of darkness But, this was the 1950s, and suburban neighborhoods were safe, seldom were people threatened with any harm. Little old ladies were safe to take walks at night. The nostalgia of safe neighborhoods was embedded in each person, and this movie predicted the fate of worse things to come. Surprisingly, this veneer of happiness and safety is shattered in a split second of terror as a medically produced vampire attacks, and the intended victims are a defenseless little old lady and her dog, less than a block from their home.

Next, let us for a moment examine 1953's *Invaders from Mars*, starring Jimmy Hunt, Arthur Franz and Helena Carter. We have a nice family whose little boy sees a spaceship crash into the sandpit behind his house. Soon his loving father George (Leif Erickson) goes to the sandpit to investigate and promptly vanishes, swirling sand reveals deep holes where numerous people disappear. Soon two cops are called to investigate by Jimmy's mother Mary (Hillary Brooke), and they find a bedroom slipper and quickly disappear under the sand dunes, their fast descent a horrid surprise. Soon George returns home, but he is drastically changed. Instead of the inquisitive, open-minded father who loves his son, he is short-tempered and is prone to yelling, a perpetual frown worn on his face.

"Any chance for a cup of coffee," he asks, an emotionless blank expression on his face. "I stopped over to see Bill Wilson, in my pajamas obviously," George firmly states, end of story, a dead look and booming music on the soundtrack. Mary looks down and sees the slipper on one foot is missing. When Mary mentions the policemen she called, he frustratingly bellows, "I wish you would please mind your own business!

When Jimmy asks his father if he saw anything while investigating the sandpit, his father curtly responds, "Let's not start that flying saucer nonsense again" and there is a quick cut closeup to the back of George's neck that shows he has a transmitter embedded there, obviously not normal. A musical stinger erupts ... David asks about it and his father seems quite upset and pulls up his coat around his neck, covering it. George states twice he caught the back of the neck on barbed

A publicity shot of Jimmy Hunt and one of many Martian mutants.

wire, but when David continues to question him about it, his hand strikes David hard on the face, stunning the confused boy.

As his wife finally serves George the hot cup of coffee, the two policemen who were pulled under the swirling sand arrive on the scene. The policemen ask about George's current condition, and agree to not report the incident, allowing it to die. George tells the policemen, "You have important work to do."

Father (Leif Erickson) and son (Jimmy Hunt) before George's change.

David and Dr. Blake (Helena Carter) confront Martian mutants after falling into the sandpit behind his backyard.

(top)David inspects the transmitter embedded in the back of George's neck; (bottom) The policemen share a special bond with George, after returning from the sandpit.

"You do too," the policemen respond.

There appears a hint of an all-knowing smile that registers on George's face, unseen by anyone but the audience.

Just by circumstance David decides to watch the sandpit area with binoculars, and it just so happens the little girl David's age, Cathy, vanishes beneath the sand dunes. When David reports the incident to her mother Mrs. Wilson, upsetting her tremendously, little Cathy comes home, having picked flowers for her mother. David says, "The ground opened up and something pulled her down." Cathy's ex-

pression is emotionless and dead. David knows it is time to leave when Mrs. Wilson believes he made up the whole story. He then finds fire shooting up from the Wilson cellar, an open can of gasoline lying in the basement. Meanwhile, at the same time ominous music plays as George escorts Mary to the edge of the sandpit.

What can be more familiar than the warm feelings between father and son? Then suddenly the father changes becoming a moody beast, shouting and physically striking his son with very little provocation. He demands obedience from his

wife and has an unexplained bond with the two policemen returning from the backyard sandpit. Speaking of backyards, isn't there supposed to be a sense of sanctuary there, a place where you can play and daydream and not worry about the dangers of the outside world? And certainly not fret about a neighbors' cellar going up in flames or a Martian spaceship landing beneath the backyard.

Thirdly, let's look at *Invasion of the Body Snatchers*, a film like *Invaders from Mars*, in that it deals with close relatives who rapidly change and are different. Not in a physical sense, but in an emotional one. The friend or loved one seems to be distant and not acting as they normally would. They are pretending to be themselves but are actually someone or *something* else.

As the sequence opens, Becky and Dr. Miles meet again after many years, Both are now divorced, Becky tells Miles that her cousin Wilma (Virginia Christine) believes that her Uncle Ira is an imposter, somebody that only looks like him. Miles tells Becky that Ira is his patient and he will stop over at Ira's to investigate.

Meanwhile closing the office for the day, Ira, little Jimmy Grimaldi and his grandmother burst into Dr. Miles' office, Jimmy quite hysterical. The doctor tells Jimmy to calm down, that everything will be all right. But the young boy bursts free, crying, most upset. The nurse must hold him. Miles thinks it is school which bothers him, but the grandmother says that's not the problem, it is that Jimmy thinks my daughter-in-law is not his mother. "She isn't, she isn't … don't let her get me!" Jimmy screams as he fights to get away from the nurse. Miles beckons the grandmother out of the room, asks if Jimmy could stay with her, and orders

Uncle Ira (Tom Fadden), or is it?

Becky (Dana Wynter), Miles (Kevin Mc-Carthy) and Wilma (Virginia Christine)

Miles eventually gets caught up in the terror of ordinary places and things.

her to give him pills several times a day as Jimmy cries out he won't stay with his mother.

After speaking alone to Ira, he sees Becky and Wilma lounging behind Uncle Ira's home. Miles tells the girls that it is Uncle Ira, all right. Wilma, concerned, tells Miles with some certainty, "He is not!" Miles watches as Ira cuts the grass. He asks, "How is he different?"

Wilma answers, "There is no difference you can actually see. He looks, sounds, acts and remembers like Uncle Ira."

"Then he is your Uncle Ira."

"But there's something missing. When he talked to me, there was a special look in

his eye. That special look is gone. Wilma goes on to state his memory is just fine, that he remembers everything just fine.

"There's no emotion, none, just the pretense of it! Everything is just the same, but not the feeling. He's not Uncle Ira."

Miles tries to convince Wilma that the trouble is within her. To which Wilma replies, "Am I going crazy." Miles assures her she is not. But Miles is further distracted by patients who are desperate to see him immediately and then cancel their appointments. They claim they wanted to see him for what amounted to nothing.

Once again, there is a special bond between an uncle and niece. Wilma, who has been close to Ira, knows that Ira is different, that the special spark that existed between the two is now gone, that Ira is simply not Ira any longer. He looks and acts the same, remembers the same facts, but the emotional bond that existed between the two is gone.

In both *Invasion of the Body Snatchers* and *Invaders from Mars*, close relatives look like themselves but are not acting the same. Family and friends realize that something is not right—their personality is different. The eternal spark that is the essence of George or Uncle Ira is gone. They might look the same, but they are not themselves.

Our next film *The Return of Dracula*, released by United Artists in 1958, starring Francis Lederer, Norma Eberhardt, and Gage Clarke, is an apple pie horror film where the king of the vampires festers within the little town of Carleton.

He's got the crazy idea she isn't his mother.

Jimmy Grimaldi is sure his mother is not his mother.

In one pivotal sequence, about the seven-minute mark, the family is gathering at the train depot to pick up their European Cousin Bellac, to them a very worldly man, to us the dreaded Count Dracula.

Mickey Mayberry (Jimmy Baird) is up in the hills behind his house looking in abandoned mines for his pet cat. He roams through the rolling hills and caves calling out "Nugget" before finding the lost cat in a mining pit. Tending to the cat, he hears the train whistle blow, signaling Cousin Bellac is soon to arrive and he better head for home immediately. He'll return for the cat later.

A quick cut to the train depot reveals the train is about 20 minutes early, a rare occurrence in Carleton. Cut back

Cousin Bellac (Francis Lederer), Cora (Greta Granstedt), Tim (Ray Stricklyn), Mickey (Jimmy Baird) and Rachel (Norma Eberhardt)

Cousin Bellac or Count Dracula

to Mickey finding his friend (and teenage heartthrob) Tim (Ray Stricklyn), who is waxing his convertible in front of a home with well-manicured hedges, a stone wall, and white picket fence. Tim tells Mickey you better tell the family that the train is arriving early. Mother Cora (Greta Granstedt) is busy sewing and Mickey tells her that the train is ahead of time, but the overwhelmed mother tells her son the train is not due for half-an-hour. She gets her coat and looks in the mirror to adjust her hat, essential for every mother in that era, as daughter Rachel (Norma Eberhardt) comes running down the stairs. They try to get in a good position in front of the mirror, as mother states, "I hope he likes asparagus with cheese."

In a single shot, the quaint house, the white picket fence, the boyfriend, the son, mother and teenage daughter

are caught in the same shot. They all rush into the car and speed to the train station. The depot men say no passengers were on the train, but Bellac suddenly appears out of nowhere and the mother, children and Bellac exchange pleasantries about the past. Arriving home, as the family moves inside, Bellac goes on and on about the very quaint house of Cora's that reminds him of the Old World. Cora says it will be grand to have a man around the house. Tim asks to see Rachel later, but she says she can't since the reverend is coming for diner.

Even though everything seems cozy on the surface, there remains hints of an invasion from the Old World vs. the New One, Count Dracula relocating from a ravished world and finding fresh blood in America. The innocence of America

and love of all things familiar are being attacked by a polluting evil.

In this swift five-and-a-half-minute sequence we have an overkill of 1950s Americana: the quaint houses, the fences, the stereotypical American family, the pet cat, the sewing, the convertible, the mentioning of the reverend, hedges, the woman's hat, asparagus with cheese, talking of the good old days, etc. Into this piece of nostalgia comes the fiendish Bellac Gordal, who has already killed the real Cousin Bellac on the train and assumed his identity. He intends to continue his campaign of vampirism in fresh terrain by living in small-town America, where little is known of Count Dracula.

In another scene, Jennie (Virginia Vincent) is a patient in the Mission

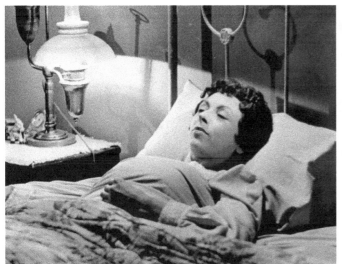

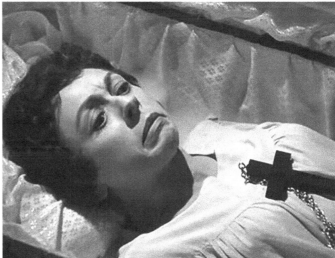

Jennie the blind girl (Virginia Vincent) in bed, and after she dies, in her coffin, paralyzed by the crucifix,

The British title for *Blood of Dracula*

Dracula materializes in a cloud of mist outside Jennie's room.

House, a church-sponsored home for the infirm and elderly. When Rachel arrives for her weekly volunteer night at the Mission house, the Rev. Dr. Whitfield (Gage Clarke) tells her that Jennie has been ill and asking for her. Rachel is very concerned about Jennie, a late-20ish brunette who is blind.

Rachel enters Jennie's room and starts chatting with her. She asks Rachel if Bellac has arrived. The young woman goes on and on about how wonderful he is. She continues reading a romance novel to Jennie and the two discuss the book. Suddenly Jennie turns serious, and while holding Rachel's hand she confesses the feeling that she will die this very day. She says some nights are darker, even black, and she is so afraid of being alone. A dog howls loudly outside, or is it a dog? Jennie thinks she hears somebody at the window, but Rachel says it's only the wind blowing, that she will close it just a little. Then Rachel continues reading the novel aloud until Jennie falls asleep. Rachel takes a small black crucifix from Jennie's fingers.

After Rachel leaves, Dr. Whitfield enters the room to check on Jennie. When he leaves a mist forms outside the window and Count Dracula/Bellac materializes. The girl, half awake, asks, "What did you say?"

Dracula responds, "I said look at me Jennie. Open your eyes and look at me. You can see me if you try. See me with your mind. I can free your soul, Jennie. I can take you from the blackness into the light. Look at me, Jennie. Can you see me now?"

Jennie, now fully awake, opens her eyes wider and says, "Yes!"

Dracula descends for the vampire's fatal kiss.

This metaphor is so extreme. Count Dracula is the wise, older European man, while Jennie is the young, naïve innocent girl. Even though he lives in darkness, he tells Jennie he can take her into the light from the blackness and she can see again. He seduces her with promises of restoring her sight so she can emerge into the sunlight.

All is familiar and nostalgic in Carleton, and life is good. The church's Mission house is center of the community. People volunteer to help one another. But into this God-fearing small town comes Old World evil that threatens to destroy the community from within. The horror of the familiar favors Count Dracula and his corruption.

Our next film is American International's *Blood of Dracula* starring Sandra Harrison, Louise Lewis and Gail Ganley. This movie puts a twist on the horror of the familiar. Instead of showing a lily-white nostalgic America, it begins by stripping it all away. This girl, Nancy Perkins (Sandra Harrison), must learn to survive in a new, less satisfying world. The horror results from her rejecting this new life and struggling to return to the old one. To do so she bonds with one of the teachers in her new boarding school, Miss Branding (Louise Lewis), a teacher who plans to turn her into a monster. The horror results from this rebellion.

The first few minutes of the movie shows a car speeding through the night, rain pouring down, tension inside. We meet the father, the new stepmother and the conflicted daughter, Nancy Perkins (Sandra Harrison). She seems sad and appears ready to cry. She reaches into the front seat and grabs the steering wheel from her father. The car swerves and almost crashes. The father reaches and

Stepmother (Jean Dean), Nancy (Sandra Harrison), and Dad (Thomas B. Henry) fighting.

Nancy's anger-management issues see her transformed into a vampire by her science teacher.

hits her in the face. "Are you out of your mind?" She now cries.

"Give her another one … what a way to go, I really thought we had it," the terrified stepmother says.

"I warned you at home. I don't want to really go there," bellows the daughter.

"Well, you have to!" demands the father.

"You can take me there, but I won't stay," Nancy yells back at him

"Whew, you could have killed us all," the father utters.

"That's what I tried to do," Nancy says matter of fact.

"The kid lost her marbles. Talking wild like that. Paul, I'm certainly glad we are getting rid of her," the stepmother proclaims.

"Shut up!!!" Nancy explodes.

"That's no way to talk to your stepmother," the father instructs.

"Mother … my mother's dead," she corrects her father.

"Oh, you're back on that track," the father says.

"And I'll never get off!" Nancy makes clear, lighting a cigarette.

"I don't approve of your smoking, but I guess one more can't hurt you now," the father says bending back to light Nancy's cigarette.

"Let her have a whole pack if it will calm her nerves," the stepmother offers.

Nancy and the headmistress (Mary Adams) argue.

"I'll handle this, dear. Now look Nancy. We discussed this back and forth."

"Then you ought to know how I feel," Nancy pleads.

"You ought to see it my way. I have a right to re-marry," the father tries to explain.

"You're on that lonesome kick once again … at least you could have waited. Six weeks and you married … her," Nancy sneers.

"You're selfish. Maybe your mother spoiled you. All you think of is yourself," the father testifies.

"Me! You're a fine one to talk. You sell the house, yank me out of school, you break my whole social life. I lose all my friends, especially Glen when we are getting close … you break it up and now you are trying to get rid of me," Nancy lashes out.

"Did you expect us to take you along on our honeymoon?" the stepmother adds.

"You put a ring through Dad's nose …" Nancy declares.

"That will do," Dad shuts the argument down.

Instead of embracing only the good life, Nancy is forced to abandon it. She loves her school with all her friends, her boyfriend Glen, her social life, but now she feels abandoned, as though her father and new stepmother want to get rid of her. Her father even strikes her in the face. She is being placed in a boarding house and must adjust to new cliques and friends. Her father is not the loving kind and can't wait to get rid of Nancy; her stepmother is more the witch from fairy tales, not the girl's best friend (who openly admits in front of Nancy she wants to get rid of her). She becomes the new wife six

weeks after the death of Nancy's mother. In this film marriage is described as a ring through his nose, as though marriage exists only to control an individual. The wholesome warm and fuzzy world of the 1950s is being turned on its ear and thus horror is allowed to tarnish an idyllic world that no longer exists.

Our final example is Hammer's *The Horror of Dracula*. One instance quite nicely illustrates the horror of familiar, a rather short one. It involves Dr. Van Helsing (Peter Cushing) and Holmwood (Mi-

Count Dracula (Christopher Lee) and victim Melissa Stribling

tinues his patrol. The worried husband believes Mina is protected and safe. Time passes, morning arrives, and the men enter the house. "Mina's safe now, but we must stand watch tonight, better get some rest." Van Helsing says.

"But what about you?" Holmwood answers.

"I'll be all right in there, if I may," Van Helsing suggests.

While Van Helsing waits below, Arthur Holmwood goes upstairs, uttering a loud "Mina," as he finds his wife sprawled on the bed. Blood running down her shoulder, Mina is near death.

The point of this scene is that our heroes have been tricked into guarding against the threat outside when the evil emanates from the inside. One feels safe in one's home, the cozy environment promotes a sense of well-being and comfort. But Count Dracula taints the safe place from within. He knows exactly where humans are most vulnerable—when weakened by a false security. They do not expect the impending horror. Dracula must be where one least expects him. He must hide amid the vestiges of the familiar, where horror is least suspected. Dracula is a crafty devil! Evil is hiding inside, in things that comfort us—and the great unknown, the outside, is no longer a threat, but people still believe it might be.

So, we see that evil is among familiar things. Those things and places and even people that bring such joy, love, and comfort may be harboring multitudes of evil, unsuspected. In sweet, huggable nostalgia may lie ultimate evil. We can't afford to let our guard down, because evil is prepared to leap out full force. The horror of the familiar will strike where and when we least expect it. It lurks in all the safe places.

chael Gough) standing guard over Mina (Melissa Stribling), who is very weak and anemic. Van Helsing is patrolling the outside of the house, slowly walking, his eyes taking everything in. He encounters the worried Holmwood, also keeping guard, carrying a crucifix for extra protection. Mina, inside, goes to the window to check on her men, but then she advances toward the bedroom door. With both a look of anticipation and dread, she opens the bedroom door and encounters the deadly Count. Dracula slowly and solemnly comes up the staircase as Mina beckons him. Closing the door with a slam, he approaches Mina, who sits on the bed as Dracula sits next to her and offers a welcoming smile. She continues to be afraid, yet her face expresses a deep desire. When the alluring creature of dark-

ness nuzzles her neck and goes in for the vampire's kiss. An owl screeches outside as Holmwood jerks around in shock. He smiles, realizing it's only an owl and con-

THE PHANTOM OF THE MONASTERY

FLYING UNDER THE RADAR

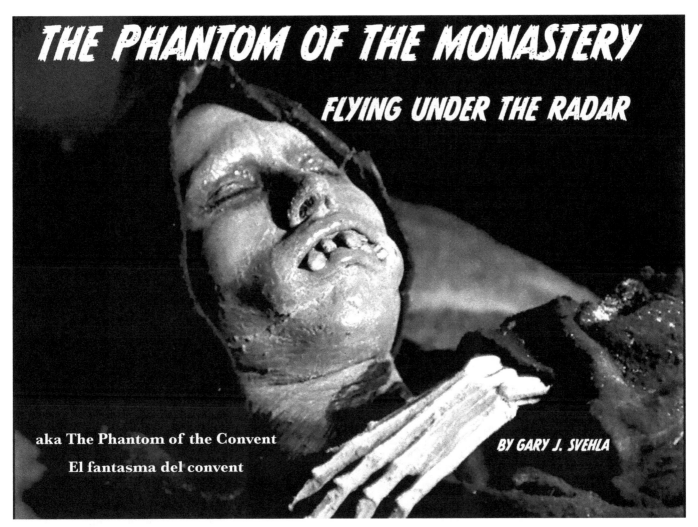

aka The Phantom of the Convent

El fantasma del convent

BY GARY J. SVEHLA

In today's world, almost every movie has been examined many times over, but a few remain such as *The Phantom of The Monastery* (1934) that formerly existed in a very gray area in the bootleg arena. But fortunately for us it has now been restored and released to the mainstream market. In other words, there are a few decades-old films awaiting examination for almost the first time. We all know of the Mexican *Dracula* that was concurrently filmed with the American Tod Browning/Bela Lugosi classic, but while it was filmed in Spanish with a foreign cast and crew, it was still a Universal production with American financing. But what of other Mexican films filmed in Mexico with Mexican financing? The time is ripe to explore a new culture of films, since productions made in Italy, Spain, France, Germany and England have all been explored exhaustively. Now is the time to examine the world of early Mexican movies, not just the 1950s and 1960s K. Gordon Murray television releases.

We must credit the creative thinkers of Mexico that dared to tell stories and folklore. *La Llorona* tells of the Weeping Woman, a popular Mexican leg-

end. Maricruz Castro-Ricalde, from Blu-ray booklet opines: "Take *The Phantom of The Monastery*, Mexican writers and directors tried to avoid American influences and so they avoided monsters, deranged mad scientists and easy scares to create something original."

However, they could not create their movies without some influences from beyond Mexico. Filmed in 1933, Mexican culture could not help being influenced by some commonly used tropes. Here we have the introduction of a mysterious stranger and his huge dog Shadow, who

The mysterious stranger seems to resemble Bela Lugosi from *White Zombie* (right) or *Murders in the Rue Morgue.*

guide the trio of hikers to the monastery. With his all-black hat and cloak the man resembles Bela Lugosi from either *Murders in the Rue Morgue* or *White Zombie*. And when seen from behind, his cloak reminds us of Dracula's cape. In another scene our heroes see a giant bat projected on the monastery walls—the source of its illumination is unknown. The dark shadowy bat reminds us of Dracula. After three loud, slow knocks on the front door, a peering face and enraged eyes stare at us from a barred window. The scene resembles a similar one from *The Old Dark House*, where Boris Karloff does the glaring. The basic plot re-invents the Faust legend

At the bottom of a staircase the trio finds a room of empty coffins, each with dry earth inside.

As the visitors arrive at the monastery, they knock three times and peering eyes appear at the front door.

where a mysterious Brother Rodrigo sells his soul to Satan in exchange for realizing his greatest desire. At the movie's end, we ask the same question, was it all a dream or reality? The viewers are left to wonder if the monks of the monastery are alive or dead? In other words, while the screenplay by Fernando de Fuentes and Juan Bustillo Oro is original and plays as a dedicated script to Mexican religion and folklore, it does indeed show influences of American horror cinema.

Unlike American horror pictures of the time, the location and architecture of Mexican horror were different from the American icons. The monastery used in Mexican cinema is very different from American horror film old standbys the castle or haunted mansion, and *The Phantom of The Monastery* used actual locations and not man-built sets, so the monastery used could employ ornate statues on the walls and art in lush frames. The bare-bones rooms or cells used contained one wooden-framed window, a stone bed with a thin mat, an old wooden table with one burning candle, a stool and a giant rosary hanging above the bed. Once guided to the monastery, the trio is welcomed and given shelter for the night. Alfonso ignores the monks' warning and strolls outside, following long corridors, ignored by monks who took a vow of silence, he comes upon a cell with a seven-foot wooden cross blocking the door and looks up to see a sign which says, "Cursed be he who turns to flesh and forgets God" and soon he hears soulful moaning inside the room. As Alfonso leans in to hear more, a monk's hand extends and touches his shoulder.

The monk waves Alfonso away, crossing his arms while standing before the door. Alfonso meekly walks away.

The endless corridors are a visual metaphor for a giant maze of human sin—confusing and mind-numbing much like our sins that are tortuous, carry us in various directions and confuse us. In another scene leaving his cell, Eduardo walks the seemingly limitless corridors coming to an archway, where he stops in utter confusion, turns totally around and then continues, walking down darkened hallways more confused at every intersection until he locates his companions, Cristina and Alfonso.

Eduardo says, "I get lost in these damn corridors!"

"It's a real labyrinth"

"These corridors are all the same, they don't lead anywhere." They all agree to find the way out, if possible.

"These monks must be doing something bad."

The trio then finds a staircase they think they recognize and they cautiously descend, unsure of what's below. At the bottom they find a room filled with coffins, with old, dried earth inside, each empty. "These coffins appeared to have been occupied and buried for a long time." Soon Brother Monje is also descending the staircase and catches the human occupants inside.

"Leave the crypt, curious ones, and follow me. The holy Prior and brethren of this community await you."

Not knowing what to expect, the trio follow.

A monk taps Alfonso on the shoulder to wave him away from Rodrigo's cell.

A typical cell in the monastery

Alfonso (Enrique del Campo) is mesmerized by his seductress Cristina (Marta Ruel).

The Phantom of The Monastery does not feature werewolves or vampires as villains, they feature a fellowship of monks that are very scary, their human forms juxtaposed to the atmospheric settings. Even one of the men states, "… afraid of humans, no, but of monks and monastery, yes." When the three people knock three slow hits on the front entrance of the monastery, they turn around to find their guide gone, disappeared into thin air. When Brother Monje appears to greet the travelers at the door and invites them in, leaving them in the entrance way for a few minutes, Alfonso says, "A community of monks who have escaped time; they escaped everything."

Christina answers, "It feels as though we are outside space and time."

They all notice a large piece of furniture leaning forward. Alfonso goes to investigate. He sees that a piece of lumber needs to be pushed underneath it and proceeds make the repair. But as soon as they look backward, the furniture is again leaning forward.

As Brother Monje returns and leads them through the maze of corridors to their cells, they pass the silhouette of a bearded monk in his cell flogging his body with a whip and quietly moaning. When the three people stop and notice this strange scene, Brother Monje closes the cell's door. The visitors continue to follow the monk down the corridors, left and right, up the stairs, where each visitor is escorted to his/her own cell.

Alfonso exits his cell, trying to ask the monks about a meal, he approaches various brothers, "Excuse me, Father," then touches the monk on the back or speaks to gain their attention, but every one of

them continues walking silently, ignoring him. None of the monks will communicate, perhaps this is normal since they took a vow of silence. These exquisite dollies down the corridors are made ever the scarier by Max Urban's full orchestra score which accentuates drum rolls, clarinet and full orchestra. Written at the same time as the American film scores of *The Mummy*, *The Old Dark House* and *The Black Cat* we find *The Phantom of The Monaste*ry music competes favorably with all three of them. Mexican film compositions in movies at the time might very well equal most early American scores.

As the visitors go down corridors, they pass the cell of a monk moaning and flogging himself.

It is interesting to observe the religious teachings and beliefs of Eduardo and Alfonso from the beginning of the movie, where both men are introduced. Remember Mexico is a vehemently Catholic country and Catholic sin is a major concern. Cristina, Alfonso and Eduardo are three hikers who get into trouble when Eduardo falls into a ravine and Alfonso must save him by pulling him up the slope. In the darkness they find themselves lost. Eduardo is content to spend the night "in the cold mountains," but Alfonso remarks, "unless we could find the old, abandoned monastery." Then Eduardo adds quite anxiously, "Strange things happen there. I'm not going." From the start we see Alfonso is devil-may-care and Eduardo is very superstitious. Besides Alfonso, Cristina (Eduardo's wife) wants to go to the abandoned monastery. Later, when journeying to the monastery and housed in individual cells there, Eduardo almost panics and says, "We should lock ourselves in these cells! These monks, this place, all seem strange, unreal … Didn't you see all the strange things since we arrived here?" Later after hearing the story of Brother Rodrigo, Eduardo says, "There's something supernatural about all this … something dark." But Alfonso feels something "very human" is occurring, not supernatural. Even Eduardo feels the supernatural is affecting the otherwise calm Cristina. He says, "Cristina feels transformed by this environment. She is a stranger." Suddenly the mother hen Brother Monje reminds the boys that two people are not allowed in the same cell and they must "maintain silence that

One morning, at daybreak,
his friend,

No, I don't think
it was this staircase.

(top) At supper the trio hears the story of Brother Rodrigo; (middle) A corpse-like hand extends from one of the monk's sleeves; (bottom) Eduardo (Carlos Villatoro), Alfonso and Cristina, the three visitors.

reigns in this house." Interesting that the monk enters the cell with three slow knocks on the cell door (just as the hikers knocked on the monastery door).

But sin is basic to the plot, and it concerns Cristina, Eduardo, Alfonso and Brother Rodrigo. First the trio of hikers. As Alfonso leaves Eduardo's cell, Cristina tells him, "Too bad Eduardo didn't fall down the ravine." Alfonso tells her she doesn't know what she's saying. Alfonso says, "This monastery, this loneliness, I don't know what's up with me." And later Cristina has a talk with Eduardo where Eduardo says he is not staying here, that Alfonso is not as calm as he appears. Cristina utters, "Alfonso is the ideal man! So, you are jealous too … It's just something I noticed for a while."

Eduardo adds, "When Alfonso is with us, you are more aware of my big failings. Maybe we should be less intimate with him." Then suddenly a projection of a bat appears on the stone wall. Trying to touch the projection, Eduardo cannot find the source of the projected image as he further examines the image of the bat. When Eduardo waves a candle, the bat's image finally fades away.

When Alfonso returns to his own cell, after Brother Monje kicks him out of Eduardo's cell, Cristina is already there waiting for him. Alfonso is very worried Eduardo might walk in on them, but Cristina only continues to smile. She rises and tenderly touches Alfonso, and he asks what she will tell Eduardo. She answers, "The truth that I love you. That we love each other." Alfonso again tells her that she does not know what she's saying, to which Cristina tells him, "Tonight I know what I want, more than ever." Alfonso loves both Eduardo (as a best friend) and Cristina, so he is totally confused. She tells Alfonso to "Love me," but he tells her to go. "There is something infernal about you tonight." Cristina, now enraged, tells Alfonso, "You are not the man I thought you were" and leaves, returning to her cell. Soon Alfonso follows her and knocks on her door begging to be forgiven, crying, but she ignores his pleading and Alfonso walks away dejected.

Simply put, this is a major Catholic sin, desiring another man's wife and giving in to temptation. In all cultures it is condemned, but especially in Catholic

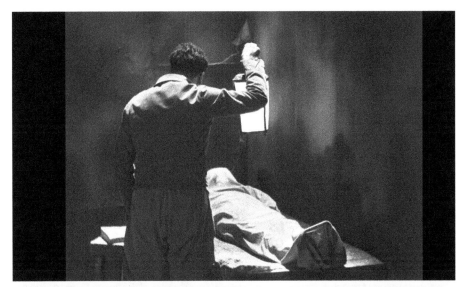

Mexico. Typically, women are the breeders of sin, the temptresses and seductresses, these evil but beautiful creatures lure men to damnation. Men are supposed to be strong and resist any temptation, showing unwavering faith to their religion.

Now the contrasting story of Brother Rodrigo and his sin is told to the trio during dinner by the Prior who tells the guests, "You've come from the world and are not bound by their vow [the monks] of chastity and poverty," so he agrees to tell them exactly what is going on. The Prior invites them for supper, to share "the bread of pain and the water of anguish." The trio of guests eat silently, looking around the room cautiously. Then to make conversation, Alfonso asks does the dog belong to the monastery and the Prior answers, "Shadow was born in the monastery and has never left it. He will accompany the Brothers of Silence forever." Then Alfonso reminds him the same dog Shadow accompanied the weird stranger who guided them to this monastery, to which The Prior answers that "Shadow never left the monastery," to which Alfonso quickly asks another question, not wishing to break into a major dispute: "How can the Brothers of Silence exist today and in this age?" The Prior at first makes funny eyes at him and then answers, "Time can do nothing in the face of things and humans that don't exist." Then since the brotherhood took a vow of silence, the Prior requests they ask no further questions.

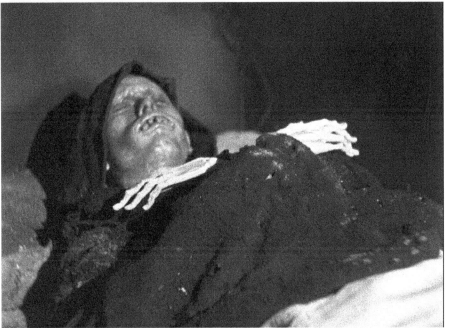

Then the sins of Alfonso, Cristina and Brother Rodrigo are cleverly intertwined as Christina interlinks her hands with Alfonso's. The Prior quickly gives a stern look of disapproval and, feeling the outrage, they quickly unlock their hands as a strong wind erupts, blowing from outside to inside, raging. The monks appear fearful and soon the window whips open. The Prior quickly rises and says, "My Brothers, our struggle is not over yet; he is getting closer; he is circling our holy house. Let us confront his curse with our faith and our prayers." Three slow knocks are heard on the wooden door (by now the three knocks are a repeated pattern) but it is only Brother Monje entering, declaring Brother Rodrigo has returned to his cell. "His wailing can be heard again." The monks all stand and leave in pairs, as the Prior opens a closet where the

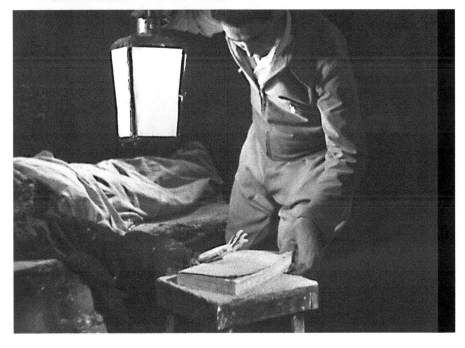

The monks leave the dinner table to give thanks to God for protecting them.

Eduardo with the reflection of the bat

Brothers are storing a statue of Christ. In ritualistic harmony, they leave, weaving through the corridors, going upstairs, to gather and pray in a room above. Cristina and Alfonso are anxious to discover what the monks are doing, while Eduardo waits behind, calling Alfonso and Cristina's attention to the monks' plates—they have no food on them—only ashes.

Now is a good time to note the superb cinematography of Ross Fisher, who creates, in 1934, a sequence reminiscent of many Val Lewton films made a decade later. Fisher can produce and extend atmosphere. In their processional walk to pray in the church upstairs, the camera captures the monks following the Prior, each monk carrying one elongated candle, with the large statue of Christ leading the procession up winding staircases and twisting throughout the building as the visitors hide behind an archway to remain unseen, the fluid camera following both the motion of the monks and the trio. This sequence is both chilling and beautifully shot.

Upstairs, the Prior places the statue of Christ on the altar and says as he shuffles through sheet music on a stand, "I will sing the mercies of the Lord in eternity from generation to generation … you have not allowed him to enter our house," the procession soon returns to the dinner table, but the guests arrive first. The Prior replaces the Christ statue in its closet and addresses the guests, "Not being able to curb your curiosity is a serious offence." As the monks return to eating (eating dust?), Eduardo sees one of the monks eat as his hand, now skeletal, extends beyond

the sleeve. In a quick second, the monk covers his bony hand. Eduardo looks on in horror.

The Prior tells the visitors the story of sin and Brother Rodrigo. "In this monastery exists a cursed cell that God has forgotten. It is a cell whose doors we have closed and protected with a cross … only after his terrible death, did we know the gravity of his offence … that God was not willing to forgive. Brother Rodrigo had desired the wife of his best friend. He desired her with all the torture of his heart and flesh … He found a book of Evil and Power … this book taught him

in exchange for his soul … he can achieve his greatest desire … he gave in to temptation, his friend lay dead in bed with the mark of Satan on his neck … He wanted to undo the pact, but it was too late [as this is being said, Christina looks lustfully at Alfonso] … Brother Rodrigo entered the monastery to live a life of austerity and penitence … Cries from Rodrigo's cell, monks tried to get in … Rodrigo was dead with the mark of the burning hand of Satan … Evil had claimed its debt … but his body never remained in its grave … His body returned to the cell as if showing us that our prayers had not managed to re-

The monks' procession carrying the statue of Christ is shown in silhouette. This accentuates the photography of Ross Fisher.

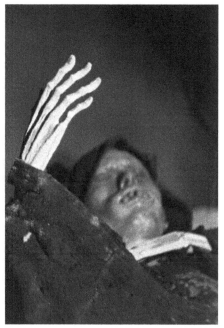

(left) A shrouded body lies on the stone bed in Rodrigo's cell; (right) The corpse under the shroud moves its hand.

deem his soul … Since then, our mission has been to save the soul of Brother Rodrigo. Until we obtain its peace, our souls won't rest." And when Rodrigo returns to his cell, moans are heard, and from his cell door, "three clear knocks resound— struck by the invisible hand of Satan."

Even though the sin of lusting after another man's wife is the same, a major difference does occur. When Cristina tells Alfonso to "love her," he tells the woman he loves to leave, he does not give in to lust or murder. When Brother Rodrigo has the chance to consummate his illicit relationship, he does, and even worse he makes the fatal pact with Satan to see his best friend die a horrible death. Strangely, the Prior sees Christina lock fingers with the man who's not her husband, Alfonso, while at dinner and he must suspect they are having an affair by the stern look on

his face, and by coincidence, he just so happens to tell the story of a similar adulterer (Rodrigo). It is as though he had the story in his hip pocket and was waiting for the moment to tell it. But coincidence is coincidence, or is it?

The centerpiece scene, after Alfonso rejects Cristina's advances but has strong second thoughts about her, has him pass Brother Rodrigo's wooden cross-blocked room and stare. He places his ear to the door to hear all he can, then the door opens, a misshapen, gnarled hand opening it slowly, darkness inside. Taking the lantern from the doorway, he enters the room. Surprisingly, the room looks like a century of dust has covered every object inside. Looking around further, he sees a shrouded body on the stone bed. As he examines the body by removing a portion of the shroud, he sees a decaying

corpse. Soon a century of dust is lifted as the corpse appears to slowly come back to life (shades of Universal's *The Mummy*). The corpse slowly lifts his arm and finally lowers his hand on an ancient book (apparently *The Book of Evil and Power*) sitting on a stool beside him. The open page of the book says, "Do not look for me on the outside, but look inside yourself, within your own heart. If you are strong, call upon me. If you call with your soul and are ready to pay the price, I will make your greatest, your most burning desire come true." Obviously, Brother Rodrigo called with his soul and paid the ultimate price, but Alfonso is still very conflicted over his relationship with both Eduardo and Cristina and moves around the room in a confused manner. Suddenly "will die" appears as giant-sized writing over the text of the book, as Alfonso

(left) Alfonso looks at the cross-barred door of cursed Rodrigo; (right) A gnarled hand opens the door to darkness.

The coffins are once more filled with ancient mummies.

finally yells "no, no" and throws the book down. Magically, the corpse hand on the stone bed has turned human, transforming into the body of Eduardo, dead. "Ask me with your soul," Alfonso tacitly remembers as his voice reflects. "Pay the price," but Alfonso only yells "no," as the front door slowly closes. Alfonso strains to open the door, panics, but only can see the corpse of Eduardo on the bed, grimacing in death. Then Alfonso tries even harder to force the door open, exerting more energy, soon collapsing onto the floor of the cell.

It is amazing that in 1934 music and art direction was so important to a Mexican horror movie. We must remember that up to now, the entire film has occurred at night and that the horror of blackness has dominated the movie, but now, after a long fade to black, we awaken to a field of light, the sun rising over meadows. We dolly into the monastery in daylight and see huge windows, ornate arches, artwork and intricate doorways. It's almost as though we have two movies here, one that occurs in darkness, another occurring in the world of light. In fact, the entire movie is one of duality: day and night, good (the tempted) and evil (the seductress, the corrupted), living and dead, dream and reality, the past and the present, the supernatural and the human and empty coffins and occupied ones.

We see that Rodrigo's door is now closed once again. We cut to the sign above the door and pan downward to see only the hand of Alfonso enter the frame from the right. Then we pan further right to see Alfonso lying unconscious outside the cell. Mysteriously, the lamp on the outside wall is now lit. Alfonso slowly re-

gains consciousness as he hears people calling his name. It is Cristina and Eduardo, Eduardo very much now alive, and Alfonso is delighted.

"So, it was a dream or nightmare!"

Cristina adds, "... it all seems like a dream to me too."

Surprisingly, the community of monks are not the villains of the piece that they seemed, they're more like red herrings, even though they are resurrected ghosts. It would be rather easy to call the spirit of Rodrigo a villain, since he is raised from the dead as a horrifying corpse, yet by appearing to tempt Alfonso with *The Book of Evil and Power*, this leads to Alfonso's redemption. Could Cristina possibly be the villain of the story, being a wily temptress and seducer? No, sin is the villain of the film, sin as simple as saying, "Thou shalt not covet thy neighbor's wife." Surprisingly, it is only Alfonso who undergoes the conversion of faith by enduring the horrors of Rodrigo's haunted cell, something Cristina did not confront, but she wakes the next morning having undergone a significant transformation. "It was a lie, and it was daytime," Alfonso tells his friends.

Looking at Eduardo, Alfonso smiles and tells him, "Thank God you are alive!" The lie he apparently refers to is the nighttime visit to Rodrigo's cell and encountering Rodrigo's corpse and Eduardo's death.

Christina, looking at Alfonso, smiles and says, "Thank god the night is over." Then she turns and looks at her Eduardo and says, "I also felt the strange influence of this monastery ... now in the light of day everything is different ... I don't know what happened to me."

It's as though the light of day has washed away the urge to sin between Alfonso and Cristina, that all the encounters of the night before also cleansed the sins of Cristina, committing to her husband and holding his hand. It as though she has been purified of all her evil urges toward Alfonso.

"Since we left the cells, we haven't seen a single monk, and this place seems more derelict since last night," Eduardo comments. They look outside the monastery, at the very trail that led them here, and see nothing but ancient ruins. Soon they see a white-haired man sweeping. He says, "How did you get in, I don't remember you. It's not visiting hours yet?" The trio says they are the guests of the monks.

The sweeper comments, "Whose guests?" The sweeper is very confused and asks, "Are you mad, are you pulling my leg?" Then he adds, "First, nobody came here last night, I sleep right next to the door and there are no Brothers or Fathers here, or anyone else. Then Christina remembers the room where they ate supper last night is directly across the corridor, and she requests it be unlocked and the three visitors be allowed in. The sweeper accommodates them but adds, "This door hasn't been opened for many years." Strangely, the room is exactly as last evening, except everything is covered in dust with broken relics and collapsing furniture. But Cristina is anxious to show them where she scratched "coward" into the table, proving they had supper there last night. Suddenly, the sweeper remembers seeing a Prior and community of monks and he offers to show them, a smile on his face. The sweeper leads them down a staircase where at the bottom they formerly found a room of dirt-filled empty coffins. Now all the coffins are filled with corpses and one of the visitors recognizes the corpse of the Prior. The sweeper tells the visitors these monks were buried for at least a century and haven't eaten dinner in a long time.

"I can't believe it, but we spent a night with the dead," Eduardo declares.

"No, we must have been hallucinating," Cristina says.

"Who knows if they came to life for a night or if we died for a night," Alfonso utters.

The sweeper kindly gives them directions to the highway and all three, now friends in the proper way, cross an arch overpass toward the highway as the music swells. It's a new day dawning.

They have all been spiritually healed.

MIDNIGHT MARQUEE

BOOK REVIEW

BY GARY J. SVEHLA

Hammer Complete: The Films, The Personnel, The Company by Howard Maxford; McFarlandbooks.com; Order 800-253-2187; 984 pages (9 x12); hardcover $95.00

Many wonderful books have been written about England's Hammer Films, but none have been $95 hardbacks.

This book is a paperweight, ready for your daily work out and capable of replacing hand-weights, and if this book could be measured by size and weight alone, it would be the book of the decade. But good books must be more than size and weight. And fortunately, it is.

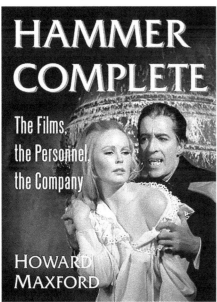

Let's examine the format of the book. First the three-column type format makes it very easy to read the small-type book and this has been a problem with aging readers and McFarland. McFarland generally features one long column of reading, and it is easy to skip a line of print or waste time reading the same line over again. This massive book is divided into: My Life with Hammer—A Rambling Introduction, The Encyclopedia, Appendix, Notes, Bibliography and Index, with most of the 1,000 pages devoted to the encyclopedia. Instead of devoting chapters to actors, production crew, the films, musicians and screenwriters, Maxford combines all of these and more into an A-Z (not just listing) compilation of sometimes small articles about people (four small-print pages are devoted to Peter Cushing), films (six pages are devoted to *Horror of Dracula* and five pages are devoted to *Dracula—Prince of Darkness*), musicians (a little less than three pages are devoted to James Bernard) and directors (over three pages are devoted to Terence Fisher). But shorter coverage is devoted to less important contributors such as Paddy Carpenter, Tommy Fletcher and Lincoln Webb, whose entries are measured in lines, but anyone who contributed to Hammer is included. From the star directors to the more modest carpenters. At first you might think the encyclopedia is a slapdash affair, but isn't it easier to research alphabetically and not worry if the person was a costume designer or set decorator? Just look up the person under their last name.

Let's look at a typical page, any page will do. So, let's pick page 568 and see what type of information is there to be found. We find small entries on people such as Maureen Moore, Patrick Moore, Robert Moore, William Moore, Trevor Morais, André Morell (the longest entry on the page), Tony Morelli, and last en-

One of the many zombies from *The Plague of the Zombies*

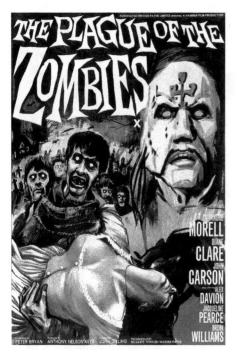

A British poster

try Charles Morgan. Now, beside André Morell, you probably haven't heard of the other names, but they are bit players, effects assistants and musicians who deserve credit for the Hammer films in which they participated. Just because every name is not familiar to fans doesn't mean their contribution is any less. The encyclopedia is loaded with excellent photos, some common and some extremely rare. The research is beyond the ordinary and is generally exhaustive, filled with new and old information. As Howard Maxford explains, this book is not made to be read page-by-page but is meant to be read as small chunks of information, as a reference tool to be explored when needed or when interested.

Looking closely at one specific entry, let's examine what Maxford writes about *The Plague of the Zombies*, one of Hammer's smaller films, held in great renown. It is very satisfying to see over three pages of coverage containing seven photos. Maxford first mentions that Hammer filmed four productions back-to-back, and *Plague* followed one week after *Dracula—Prince of Darkness* and *Rasputin—The Mad Monk* wrapped. Dracula's castle in *Prince* was converted to a Russian winter palace for *Rasputin*. "The castle was stripped of its cladding and re-dressed as quaint Cornish cottages." Maxford tells us the screenplay was written by Peter Bryan, who wrote *The Brides of Dracula* and *The Hound of the Baskervilles*. The film was known by various titles such as *The Zombie* and *Horror of the Zombie(s)*, reaching its fi-

nal title one month before filming began. Anthony Hinds was brought in to polish the script before the film went in front of the cameras. Maxford compares the script to Bryant's earlier *Hound of the Baskervilles*. Recounting the scenario briefly, Maxford calls *The Plague of the Zombies* "a minor gem." He praises director John Gilling who directed "with pace and style," working closely with cameraman Arthur Grant, "Gilling presents the action in a series of inventively framed and tightly edited shots." Then he praises several specific shots and says André Morrell was "the main asset" who brings "a genuine sense of class to his role of Sir James." He is not so kind to the film's other performers. And this is only the first page of three, citing the good and bad of every aspect of the film. Maxford even tells where one can buy the soundtrack. He also includes complete cast and credits and when the film was issued on home disc. In other words, the author Howard Maxford is way beyond exhaustive in his detailed coverage of the movie.

Next, let us explore the Appendix, another A-Z entry of all the Hammer productions which never were made. Some entries are well publicized, but many were seldom mentioned. Titles such as *Brainstorm*, *Children of The Wolf*, *The Criminal*, *Dead of Night*, *The Disciple of Dracula*, *Dracula's Feast of Blood*, *The Picture of Dorian Gray* and *Rosemary's Baby*. At least one paragraph is dedicated to each project and the reason the production failed. For instance, did you know that Hammer wanted to aquire the rights to the best-selling novel *Rosemary's Baby* by Ira Levin—it was suggested to Hammer in 1967 by Terence Fisher and immediately rejected by the studio. It was ultimately picked up by Paramount and became a major hit for Roman Polanski in 1968. Hammer also wanted to film *The Rocky Horror Show*, under the production of

Stones of Evil, one of the scores of Hammer films left unmade.

Italian poster for *The Plague of the Zombies*

Michael Carreras, but Carreras couldn't secure the needed American financing in time and was beat to the punch. Last, Hammer was approached with a script called *Dracula's Feast of Blood* by Kevin Francis and it was immediately rejected by James Carreras and Brian Lawrence, although elements from the script found their way into Hammer's *Taste the Blood of Dracula*, for which the company had to compensate Francis.

The Notes section and Bibliography sections share the various sources where Maxford got some of his information. And he seems to be a very honest author.

You can tell by now this is much more than an A-Z guide to all things Hammer. It is a well-researched tome worthy of the price being near $100. It is awfully bulky, and a Kindle or Apple e-book is probably preferred and will save your lap a great deal of strain. Besides this unavoidable problem, the book comes with the highest recommendation.

"Twice the Thrills! Twice the Chills!" by Bryan Senn; McFarland; McFarlandbooks.com; Order 800-253-2187; 423 pages (8 ½ x 11); softcover $59.95

It was years ago when writers John R. Duvoli and John Soister approached me with an idea, to write a book about horror and science fiction double features. I went for it immediately, even knowing that Duvoli and Soister were two entirely different types of writers, one very methodical and research driven, the other a newspaper writer who was succinct and loved to write from memory. That collaboration didn't last very long and the pair split, each author volunteering to do the book alone, putting me in the middle. Then enter the late great John E. Parnum, who heard about the aborted double-feature project and admitted he has been collecting ads for double-features and happily volunteered for the project. He was far along in the project when he contracted cancer of the tonsils and died before completing the book. Thank heavens author Bryan Senn independently thought of the same subject and was the first writer to complete it.

Senn's book is sensibly formatted: Acknowledgements, an Introduction, reviews of 147 double-features between 1955-1974, Appendix A: Chronology, Appendix B: Double-bills by Distributor, Bibliography and Index.

There were many reasons for double-features, chief among them the threat of television—so theatrical films added 3-D, stereophonic sound, CinemaScope and the double-feature, among other gimmicks hoping to attract moviegoers and get them back into theater seats. Senn tells us there were seven reasons the studio or film distributors created the need for the double-feature First, there were films produced and distributed by the same company; second, two films produced independently but brought together by a single distribution company; a new film released with an older picture, sometimes disguised under a different title, and packaged together by a single distributor; two reissues paired together, sometimes retitled to appear new; two pictures paired locally by a theater, theater chain, or dis-

The little independent film of Jack H. Harris, *The Blob*, invades the Colonial theater, which is playing a Bela Lugosi movie.

tributor, but only done in local areas. The book, Senn tells us, will only cover the first two types of double-features. Though double features thrived in the middle 1950s to the end of the 1970s, they date back further than that. Senn considers the double pairing of *Frankenstein* and *Dracula* in 1938 the most important double-feature ever released, but he also attributes the 1952 re-release of *King Kong* and Val Lewton's *The Leopard Man* to be very influential to the double-bill genre.

Since 1958 was a very important year for the double-bill genre, let's randomly pick one double-feature to investigate. In this case, *The Blob* and *I Married a Monster from Outer Space* to see just how Senn handles discussing double-features and how he handles the movies discussed. He first starts with detailing how director Gene Fowler, Jr. just came off a financial hit, *I Was a Teenage Werewolf*, and Paramount wanted to replicate that success. They slotted him to make *I Married a Monster from Outer Space* and decided to pair its release with an independent project they just picked up from distributor-turned-producer, Jack H. Harris, *The Blob*. Thus, the creation of a a great "match made in '50s sci-fi heaven," Senn details how Jack H. Harris of *The Blob* did not get along with 27-year-old teenager Steven McQueen and their relationship was very difficult. He could have had McQueen in his follow-up feature but considered McQueen too much of a "pain" to work with again. But Senn documents how so much later, when McQueen was dying of cancer in Mexico in 1980, only one thing decorated his room, a poster of *The Blob*.

Paramount wisely chose to place *I Married a Monster from Outer Space* as sup-

port to The *Blob*, making an independent feature top-lined over their own Paramount product. Money always seemed to talk louder than pride. While his acting was subtle and superior to his cast mates, Steve McQueen was more appreciated for his dramatic pauses, biting his lip and trying to submit a realistic performance, but he went behind the scenes and frequently argued with director Irvin Yeaworth about his interpretation of specific scenes in the script. It seemed everyone loved his emotive acting, but few loved Steve McQueen. But Yeaworth said in a small movie with a tight budget, very little could be done to accommodate him.

On the other hand, Senn considers *I Married a Monster from Outer Space* to be an "intelligent, polished gem among so much rough-cut 1950s science fiction dross," Senn complements the "multi-layered script, impressive monsters, involving direction and believable performances"

As the old man finds, nothing can be more dangerous than a blob on a stick.

A publicity shot of *I Married a Monster from Outer Space* featuring Tom Tryon, Charles Gemora and Gloria Talbott.

(especially Gloria Talbott's). Interestingly, Senn devotes time to director Gene Fowler, Jr., Gloria Talbott saying that he puts himself up on the screen, that he took the movie home every night "and slept with the script." Gloria could tell he was tired by the end of the movie and Bryan Senn states it was sad he only made seven movies in the late 1950s, before returning to editing movies.

British quad from *I Married a Monster from Outer Space*

The chapter ends with the main credits, the release date, and people who contributed quotes from published sources.

As readers can tell, Senn puts everything he can into a critique of each film and the book is filled with interesting anecdotes. The book is well researched and becomes a highly readable and enjoyable book. Well worth the 60 bucks.

American International Pictures: A Comprehensive Filmography by Rob Craig; McFarland mcfarlandbooks. com; Order 800-253-2187; 443 pages (8 ½ x 11); softcover $75.00

During the period of the 1950s and 1960s (and most of the 1970s, but to a lesser degree), there was nothing more exciting than seeing a new American International at your local theater or drive-in. We traveled with AIP through the low-budget black-and-white features which soon morphed into the colorful, widescreen films of the 1960s.

As author Rob Craig states in his Introduction: "In short, the AIP films not only thrilled and entertained us, but *changed* us—in some ways even defined us—becoming important biographical events, helping us discover our true loyalties and passions."

Craig admits other books on AIP offered their history and other information, so he didn't want to duplicate the same material, so this book offers only a complete filmography with each film critiqued. This is amply accomplished in a 400-page book, well-illustrated with ads and photos, and is so much fun to read. Wisely, Craig keeps the film synopses (press and self-written) to a bare-bones minimum, offering only a sentence or two to retell the plot of every movie.

As Rob Craig tells us in his Preface, he came late to the game, calling *Master of The World* his first theatrical viewing experience of watching AIP films. He admits to discovering AIP via television and cable TV citing *Warning from Space* as the first AIP he caught on the tube. But he feels subjective criticism is paramount. "It is thus a dangerous sign of cultural atrophy when film analysis and criticism degenerates into some form of consensus reality, which usually boils down to the death-knell of intellectual freedom." In his Introduction, Craig first gives credit to Mark Thomas McGee and Gary A. Smith for writing defining books about American International Pictures, and he admits he stands upon their shoulders. He goes on to define the filmography, stating that co-founders James H. Nicholson and Samuel Z. Arkoff's independent films after leaving AIP are also covered here. He states how the book is composed of two parts, a brief history of AIP, how the company was formed as American Releasing Corpora-

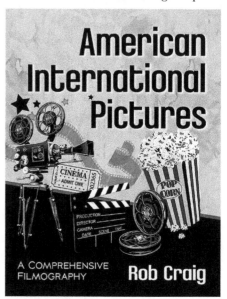

American International Pictures

A COMPREHENSIVE FILMOGRAPHY   Rob Craig

Samuel Z. Arkoff (left) and James H. Nicholson, co-presidents of AIP.

tion in 1954 and soon morphed into the familiar American International Pictures in 1956. Craig obviously did a great deal of detective work to establish a thorough history of AIP involving distribution and production companies such as American International Television (and the era of Larry Buchanans' AIP remakes), Alta Vista Productions, American International Export Corporation, American Releasing Corporation, Anglo-Amalgamated Film Distributions, Cinerama Releasing Corporation, Commonwealth United Entertainment, Trans-American Films, and several others.

But most of the book is devoted to the Filmography. So let me pick three films for discussion, one a foreign import, *Black Sunday*, and another two studio-made, *The*

Italian lobby card from *Black Sunday*

House of Usher and *I Was a Teenage Werewolf*. First, let's explore *Black Sunday*. Besides basic cast and credit information, we see that this film is production #6015. According to Samuel Arkoff's biography, he and Nicholson were highly impressed with Mario Bava's initial feature *Mask of the Satan* aka *Black Sunday*, seeing it at 8 a.m. on his way in to an unheated screening room. Craig goes on to to his personal analysis, which covers the rest of the content.

Well, I see nothing new here as all the information is from a published source, except for the critique, and Craig's critique adds nothing new to critical research or interpretation. He tells us about how Bava writes simple stories, and his films feature beautiful cinematography. He praises star Barbara Steele, who plays a dual role. Craig pulls some information from the Arkoff biography again and mentions the story that Les Baxter was hired to score the American AIP version. That is about all he has to say and there is no new information added.

Let's move on to *The House of Usher*, made in 1960 and being the first AIP film in color and widescreen. Craig mentions that AIP takes on Hammer with a lavishly budgeted production, now producing one larger budgeted production instead of generating two 1950s-style black-and-white potboilers. Because of Richard Matheson's script, AIP avoids the more soap opera aspects of a typical Hammer production and aims for a "more intelligent and subtle stab at psychological horror." AIP is no longer making movies aimed at teenagers. Craig goes on to say the cast is made up of only four players, but because of Matheson's script, we hardly notice. Craig calls the color-tinted dream sequence "somewhat hackneyed" but says the fire at the end is "thrilling." He speaks of the picture's "momentous clash of wills between two generations" as a reflection of AIP's past. He speaks of the "domicile as representative of various layers of the subconscious mind," but gives a rather brief explanation (surely *The House of Usher*, being such a pivotal picture, can warrant additional space). He considers the score by Les Baxter as "pleasant but unremarkable;" he feels that Vincent Price "carries the picture, which is slow over-all," before quoting from Victoria Price's biography. Interestingly he mentions that "radio legend" Gordon McLendon (the producer of *The Killer Shrews* and *The Giant Gila Monster*) was hired to produce a radio spot for the feature. The film surprisingly made two million dollars for the company and trans-

Vincent Price and Mark Damon looking at ancestral paintings in *The House of Usher*.

mitted loud and clear that the AIP picture of the 1950s was dead.

Fortunately, I feel Rob Craig offered a much more insightful analysis of *The House of Usher* than he did for *Black Sunday*, offering a more original critique and lots of surprising information, and his personal opinions were front and center. He did a good job here.

I Was a Teenage Werewolf, unlike the first two films, harkens back to the 1950s. We know since *Warning from Space* was his first AIP film, Craig must be younger, and let's see what he thinks of an earlier AIP picture. He starts off with a press synopsis of the movie and then tells us that the double-feature of *I Was a Teenage Werewolf* and *Invasion of the Saucer Men* made two million dollars and was the big breakthrough for the troubled youth horror film, which AIP had been making for two years. Craig says, "This sure-fire mixture of juvenile delinquency, classic horror plot points, hypnosis, and age-

In most of Europe, *The House of Usher* was known as *The Fall of The The House of Usher*.

The werewolf (Michael Landon) attacks the gymnast from *I Was a Teenage Werewolf*.

regression should have been a winner, but due to producer Herman Cohen's awkward screenplay, and miscasting of the two main characters, the film falls flat as a pancake." He says Michael Landon's "whiny method performance" and Whit Bissell's "dull screen presence" really torpedo the film. Craig says the topic of troubled youth is handled in a "cliched" manner. The screenplay takes the film far too seriously for its "infantile narrative pretensions" and feels it might be the idea behind the movie, but not the actual film, which allowed the movie to leave its mark on popular culture. Craig is that type of writer.

It's quite clear that Rob Craig has personal opinions galore on this film, but

it seems to be revisionist theory and not baby boomer opinion about this beloved 1950s picture. Come on, this is not wrong, younger writers might see the flaws in this movie more than us and they are entitled to voice them. The younger generation may not hold esteemed films in such high regard as we do, and we must admit analysis can greatly vary. Seeing that Craig's opinion may counter mine only makes me more interested to read his, for a different take. This is only healthy, but I sincerely hope that he likes a range of 1950s and 1960s/1970s films and gives the earlier films a chance. For these earlier ones allowed AIP to grow and prosper.

The Creature Chronicles: Exploring the Black Lagoon Trilogy by Tom Weaver, with David Schecter and Steve Kronenberg; McFarland; mcfarlandbooks.com. Order 800-253-2187; 394 pages (8 ½ x 11); hardcover, with full color cover, $75.00

If Frankenstein's Monster and Dracula are the reigning kings of classic monsters, they reigned during and following the early 1930s and don't really belong to our generation; the one true baby boomer creature is the Gill Man, the classic monster that is owned by monster kids. It has been too long, but finally a McFarland book has arrived. The book features full-color art and photos for the front and back covers, a splash of color inside, and it is printed on "glossy" paper.

First, we have an Introduction by Julie Adams, who starred with Richard Carlson in the first and greatest *Creature* movie. Julie admits to seeing horror movies as a child and would "crouch down on the floor and peak through the two seats in front of me during the really scary parts." Later as a Universal-International contract actor, Universal made 30 films a year and Adams was approaching her 20th film when she was assigned *Creature from the Black Lagoon*, a film that might be special today; "back then it was just another movie that Universal has just assigned to me." Julie was not the only one who is shocked we are still talking about this film six decades later, because if she knew, she would have kept the white bathing suit. Julie only conjectures how the film has become a classic. "They range from the Gill Man being a tragic figure who elicits sympathy, the Beauty and the Beast aspect … the monster suit, the scary musical theme, and the well-written script." Julie continues talking about her life in 1954 and remembrances of making *Creature from the Black Lagoon*. Most Introductions in books by stars are notoriously short and rather

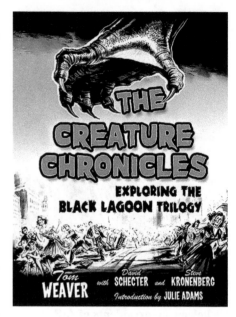

vacant, but this one is long and well-written. She brings self-reflection from a person who was there on the set.

Part One is composed of detailed coverage of *Creature from the Black Lagoon*, *Revenge of the Creature* and *The Creature Walks Among Us*, covering the bulk of the book from page 11 through page 303. Part Two covers various odds and ends such as: the Official Guide to the Sunshine State; Aquatic Kith and Kin (covering films that never would have been made if it were not for the *Creature from the Black Lagoon*); Creature Conversations; A Brief History of The Black Lagoon Bugle; and Revenge of the Return of the Remake of *Creature from the Black Lagoon*.

This is followed by Chapter Notes and Index.

Of course, we will explore the chapter on the initial *Creature from the Black Lagoon* to see what the book offers and whether the standard genre fan should buy it.

The chapter opens with the most detailed credits list ever compiled, but author Tom Weaver admits to making parenthetical but educated guesses as to what function the few uncredited people served on the production.

The seed of *Creature* started in 1940 when Orson Wells was making *Citizen Kane* and the after-dinner conversation involved two of the guests, Mexican cinematographer Gabriel Figueroa and 24-year-old William Alland, who would go on to producer status at Universal-International a decade later. Figueroa told the story of the Amazon fish people, according to Figueroa,100% true, and Alland turned the story into a three-page story idea in 1952 called *The Sea Monster*. The job of turning the story idea into a treatment

The Gill Man was the classic monster that was born of the generation of baby boomers and he belonged to us.

went to 43-year-old Maurice Zimm, a newcomer to the movies. Zimm's submission was called *Black Lagoon*. Weaver describes his treatment in detail.

The three-page treatment was critiqued in a one-page studio letter that at first praised the treatment, but then criticized it, stating the leading man was introduced too late, the stage-setting takes much too long, and there's too much of the two-character comic relief. Alland generally agreed. Alland suggested that the ending should be ambiguous so sequels could be made in the future, knowing full well the classic monster movies of the 1930s all had successful sequels. When Alland and Jack Arnold were both making

It Came from Outer Space, Maurice Zimm was busy rewriting his treatment to *Black Lagoon* as a full screenplay, heavy on his mind the studio critique. For two months another writer, Leo Lieberman, worked on what was now a script and became the missing link between Zimm and the final story fleshed out by Harry Essex, who was brought in for the final screenplay. During the time of Lieberman, screenwriter Arthur Ross was also brought to polish the evolving screenplay. About at this point they had to budget the movie and decide whether it would be 2-D, 3-D, black-and-white or color. It was first decided that the film would be budgeted at $650,000 and be filmed in Eastman color and 3-D,

but somewhere down the road the studio objected over color and *Creature* became a black-and-white production in 3-D.

But this is only page 21 of the chapter, which lasts to page 139. So, Tom Weaver has much more story to tell and always gets help from his friends, who contribute important information.

As we can see, the three writers did their homework, especially after we read the Weaver production history of each film, we get Steve Kronenberg's insightful analysis. David Schecter submits detailed critiques of the musical score of each film. Each part of the team offers his expertise.

We finally can put on our library shelf what will probably be looked upon as the definitive researched tome on three of the most important horror/monster films of our generation. And after this book, nothing more is needed.

Highly recommended for all lovers of *Creature* movies. But only if you like the movies and are not just a Creature fan and are so-so about the three films.

Halloween: The Changing Shape of an Iconic Series by Ernie Magnotta; self-published on Createspace by Ernie Magnotta; 380 pages (8 ½ x 11); softcover, with full color photos, as well as black-and-white ones, $49.99

It is about time we reviewed this self-published work by Ernie Magnotta, since the world of publishing is filled with people who feel it is best to cut out the middleman and design and publish the book yourself. To be honest, Magnotta has done a pretty good job of it, sporting a superior and subtle cover, adding many color photos, and adding much needed detail to his coverage. But upon closer examination, the book features text spaced a little too wide and the graphic design features photos not comfortably integrated with the text, having devoted too much

Julie Adams and the Gill Man from *Creature from the Black Lagoon*

Donald Pleasence as Dr. Sam Loomis, the Van Helsing character of *Halloween*

Jamie Lee Curtis, armed with a knife, is ready to attack any shape.

Judith Myers, killed and displayed by The Shape, with more victims on his agenda.

white space for the photos, appearing a little like a novice design. A real publisher could have helped here.

I am grateful for the thanks Magnottta gives Sue and me and Midnight Marquee Press, but I am sure Magnotta will greatly benefit from the criticism we offer and hope there's no hard feelings here. The first choice Magnotta made was to delete *Halloween. III: Season of the Witch* from the book simply because it does not feature The Shape as all the other films in the series do. I agree with the decision but feel Magnotta should have explained his reasons why—because of the confusion I am sure the decision caused. Suppose I wrote a book on the Universal Frankenstein series and left *Abbott and Costello Meet Frankenstein* out of the discussion, with minimal explanation why, readers would certainly expect a detailed explanation.

But let's examine what Magnotta says about the first *Halloween* film, which which occupies pages 29 to 69, to get a general idea of the book. First off, three pages are devoted to retelling the plot of *Halloween*, one of the most familiar horror films in ages. Again, a simple paragraph will do. Among a book set inside a sea of analy-

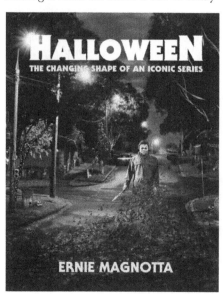

sis, if the sequels are not so well known, again a simple paragraph is all you need. The analysis of the credits sequence is very interesting because this has seldom been done, and *Halloween*'s credits are visually interesting. Then he critiques the story, but really, he is critiquing the movie. "Although *Halloween* is heavily influenced by *Psycho*, it doesn't copy Hitchock's classic." It is easy to maintain that both movies are very different, but *how* does *Psycho* influence *Halloween* besides their psychotic leading character? I do not see how one influences the other. I see them as each trying to accomplish different goals and using different styles to obtain these goals. They are simply two different genres— thriller and slasher. Maybe the same common tropes such as each killer using a butcher knife is common but using butcher knives to kill was used much earlier in movies as well.

Next Magnotta examines "Character and Acting," but with his examination of Laurie Strode (*not* Jamie Lee Curtis), his focus is more upon the character of Laurie Strode, for here he analyses the script, even referring to Laurie as the "final" girl. Jamie Lee Curtis' acting is briefly and generically profiled. Next, he likewise examines Dr. Sam Loomis as a Van Helsing

The Shape kills once again.

character, who refers to Michael as "it," "inhumanly patient" and "evil." He goes to great lengths to describe Loomis before he covers Donald Pleasence and his performance. One of many "characters" he examines is The Mask worn by The Shape and he cleverly establishes how it solidifies Michael Myer's character. Then Magnotta goes into a long analysis of "Suspense and Fear," and how it functions in *Halloween*. Then he examines "Direction and Composition" (he spends lots of time exploring Carpenter's POV shots), "Cinematography" (where he says a lot of interesting stuff about Dean Cundey's camera work and how he sets up shots for maximum suspense), "Music" (he tells us Carpenter wrote the entire score in three days) and then he stretches things a bit with "Creature of the Id" and "Theme" and finally "Evaluation." The last two headings make the book seem "schoolish," as if the book were to be written for purely academic reasons.

The problem with subheadings is they trap your thoughts. Having a very few subheadings is fine but having too many goes to show thoughts are not fully organized and they soon become tedious to the reader. For instance, could the subheading on "Suspense and Fear" be combined with "Cinematography" because Magnotta goes to show how Dean Cundey creates tension with his camera and with "Direction and Composition," how Carpenter creates suspense with his framing of the shots. Would not a combination of the three help to solidify the book?

As we can see Ernie Magnotta is new to the book-writing game and his inexperience shows. He has talent and is trying to improve, and in time he will improve. But there is nothing like an objective editor to guide you through the whole experience. You really can't do it alone … you need the whole team. That is why this is a fine book but not an outstanding one.

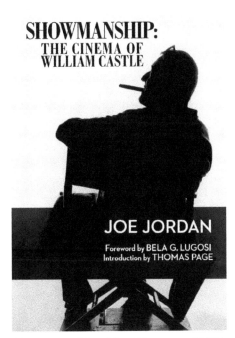

SHOWMANSHIP:
THE CINEMA OF
WILLIAM CASTLE

JOE JORDAN

Foreword by BELA G. LUGOSI
Introduction by THOMAS PAGE

Showmanship: The Cinema of William Castle by Joe Jordan; BearManor Media, PO Box 71426, Albany, Georgia 31708, www.bearmanormedia.com; 396 pages (6x9 inches); softcover, $26.95

BearManor Media are good friends with Midnight Marquee, Inc. and, like MidMar, attempt to sell books at the most affordable price. They operate out of Georgia with owner Ben Ohmart living and working with his wife in Japan.

One of their books which interested me was *Showmanship: The Cinema of William Castle*, featuring a Foreword by Bela G. Lugosi, Bela's son, where he praises Joe Jordan's passion and meticulous research. He states how Bela Lugosi gave Castle his first job in the entertainment world when he hired him for a stage job in the road show tour of *Dracula*. This book includes every film Castle directed before *Macabre* in Part One and all the famous William Castle films beginning with *Macabre* in Part Two.

But first the Introduction by Thomas Page which presents in three pages a brief biography of William Castle's style and career.

The first part explores 39 features that Castle directed before anyone knew his name. These features are all programmers, B-films, Westerns, popular entries in film series between 1943 (with *The Chance of a Lifetime*, the first film Castle directed) to 1956 (*Uranium Boom*). But let's examine what Jordan says about his fifth film, *When Strangers Marry*, made in 1944, a random entry selected because it's a film I enjoy very much.

Jordan tells us that the King brothers moved from Chicago to California

Kim Hunter in a moody shot from *When Strangers Marry*

to enter film production after dabbling in vending machines and film projector manufacturing. When first forming their film production company, Columbia president Harry Cohn allowed the brothers to have a private showing of William Castle's *The Whistler*, of which they were very impressed, and when they asked about borrowing Castle for their new movie, Cohn charged them five times the rate of his current weekly salary, which they happily agreed to. Then Jordan offers a brief synopsis, before the film is critiqued. Jordan states it was difficult to replicate success in back-to-back films, but Castle wanted to show America what he could offer. Jordan says Castle's work on the picture is comparable to the work of Hitchcock, but at first, he only refers to Castle's cameo appearance in a photograph, the gimmicky

One of the earlier roles of Robert Mitchum, *When Strangers Marry*

A newspaper headline from *When Strangers Marry*

side of Hitchcock and not true style. He makes a case that finding the Silk Stalking Murderer compares to finding a MacGuffin, a desired object pursued by the main characters in some Hitchcock films. He then makes another case that Castle is trying to explore the American "melting pot" by hosting the narrative in the city of brotherly love, Philadelphia. Then he specifically examines a Turkish bath scene (one minute long) in the hotel as being an example of this "melting pot."

Hogwash!

Anyone trying to make the case that William Castle's talent even remotely approaches or even imitates the talent of Hitchcock is delusional. I love Castle but accept him on his own level of talent, but what elevates him to the academy of the greats, such as Hitchcock, is indeed an over-stretch and becomes silly. And who the heck cares about the American "melting pot" in B-Castle films? It's as though Jordan was a student who just learned the concept and was trying to impress his teacher by using it in his next theme. But instead of leaving well enough alone, Jordan introduces the concept of "salad bowl." Then—and much too briefly—Jordan tells us about a few interesting scenes. Jordan mentions aspects of those scenes that Castle would use in his more popular movies to come. Nice touch. Jordan mentions what a great director William Castle was but only notes his gimmicky use of clever transitions as an example, but this was probably the work of the film editor and *not* Castle. Then he ends the chapter with the film's premiere. But tell me, why aren't stars such as Kim Hunter and Robert Mitchum explored in more depth since Jordan goes out of his way to show a photograph of Robert Mitchum's sister in his coverage of *House on Haunted Hill*? Why is it not mentioned that the film was re-released as *Betrayed*? Why does he spell

Annabelle (Carol Ohmart) is terrorized by the apparently living skeleton from *House on Haunted Hill*.

Vincent Price is the murderer in *House on Haunted Hill*.

Mrs. Slides (and not the preferred spelling *Slydes*)?

Next let's randomly examine a film from the second part of the book, my favorite being *House on Haunted Hill*, released in 1958, page 221 to page 244. Jordan begins by adding a dash of production information before going into familiar territory with the development of EMERGO. Then there is a one-paragraph scenario of the movie. Followed by another nugget of info when Vincent Price admits liking the story, committing to the movie. The analysis is all over the place and seems to

be coming at the reader from all directions. He next cleverly talks about the intensity Castle makes the actors commit to and cites the performance of Elisha Cook, Jr. as a good example. Jordan discusses the various characters in depth calling Nora "the most fragile of the film characters" and states her encounter with Mrs. Slydes works so effectively because of her fragile vulnerability. Jordan cleverly points out that this is a tale of a man murdering his wife disguised as a ghost story. Then more rambling analysis occurs before Jordan relates Hollywood's Louella Parsons' ap-

pearance at the premiere, suggesting that she could make-or-break movies before release. Happily, Parsons had nothing but good things to say about the movie. The film went on to become a hit, making low-budget horror films was becoming his specialty. And William Castle was now ready for his best film, according to Jordan, *The Tingler*.

There exists a kernel of good information on William Castle within the book but sadly the "melting pot" examples and the Hitchcock comparisons are not one of them. The title refers to gimmicks used in his films, but when Jordan refers to clever transitions used in *When Strangers Marry*, he never refers to the gimmicky effect of

those edits on the viewing public. And when mentioning the use of Castle's cameo in the photograph in the same film, Jordan never plays up the gimmicky effect of playfully copying Hitchcock's style. Jordan sees plenty of gimmicks in the Castle films he watches, but he either ignores such gimmicks or woefully plays them down (the EMERGO coverage). And I partially blame his editor for not catching things to tell him to either cut or expand. The author always needs help, and he wasn't given enough, or else he ignored it.

Mrs. Slydes (Leona Anderson) confronts Nora (Carolyn Craig) in *House on Haunted Hill*.

MIDNIGHT MARQUEE

MOVIE REVIEW

BY GARY J. SVEHLA

Each issue of Midnight Marquee we compile a few movie reviews that, for various reasons, never get published and they then sit around, waiting to get into print. At the same time, a film is waiting for another review that is being released for perhaps the fifth time in 4K, or unless you are a DVD BEAVER fanatic (a terrific website that is a must for all film fans), what is the point of reviewing the movie once again? What can you possibly say that is new and matters? So, this issue we are discontinuing reviewing the latest releases that were already reviewed multiple times and publishing those reviews that have been sitting around the office much too long.

1.0	POOR
2.0	FAIR
3.0	GOOD
4.0	VERY GOOD
5.0	EXCELLENT

THE INVASION [2.0]

Amazingly, Jack Finney's novel *The Body Snatchers* has now been filmed four times (*Invasion of the Body Snatchers* [1956]; *Invasion of the Body Snatchers* [1978]; *The Body Snatchers* [1993] and *The Invasion* [2007]), with the Don Siegel original being the true classic of the bunch. Most critics trashed the latest doctored version, directed by newcomer Oliver Hirschbiegel, whose version was considered too tame for wide-spread commer-

cial appeal. The film sat on the shelf for two years.

Rumors persist that the Wachowski brothers (of *Matrix* fame) reshot and re-cut the film's ending, making it more explosive. If they did reshoot, the film is worse off because of it, with Dr. Bennell (Nicole Kidman) driving a speeding car which is covered headlight-to-taillight with "snatchers." She zooms down the highway trying to shake off the alien hive. Shortly thereafter her car is engulfed in flames, yet Bennell still drives her car into

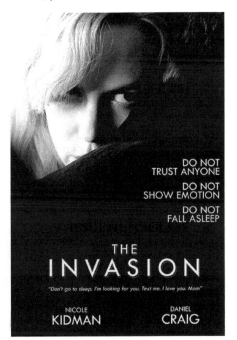

a parking garage to race to the elevator to meet a rescuing helicopter on the landing pad on top of the building. Very dramatic and explosive, flames shooting everywhere, yet very pedestrian by-the-numbers action-adventure cinema 101. I would love to see Hirshbiegel's original cut and can almost guarantee, while it might be less commercial, that it would be more artistic and satisfying.

The basic premise of all four movies revolves around invasion from space via an alien race that plans to take over the human race by turning human beings into aliens, creatures who look the same but no longer feel any emotion. Alien survival no longer involves the good of the individual but the good of the hive society. And the change from human to alien always occurs when people fall asleep. The first three movie versions involved alien pods that mimicked their human counterparts, the human shell destroyed once the alien copy was complete. In *The Invasion* pods are forgotten, as the infected humans vomit the alien virus into the mouths of intended victims, the virus ultimately replacing our human identity with the alien one during sleep.

Each movie version becomes a metaphor of fear for its time. The original Don Siegel version, occurring in Utopian Santa Mira, small-town America, involves the aliens as metaphor for Communism, the so-called Red Threat, where human emotion is erased, and the prospering commu-

Nicole Kidman and Daniel Craig from *The Invasion*

nity means more than the will of the individual. By 1978 director Philip Kaufman brought the alien invasion to the big city, San Francisco—where individual human identity was hard to maintain among such urban sprawl. Kaufman exposed counter-cultures and New Age cults as one means of maintaining a unique human identity and his film captured the terror of remaining human in such an impersonal world. *The Body Snatchers'* director Abe Ferrara's attempt to rethink the story on an American military base, focused on the paranoia of the military, with its own hive personality taking over and eliminating the will of the individual.

A space shuttle crashes to Earth carrying a virus from outer space that, during sleep, transforms human beings into this collective alien consciousness. The movie is even more releant with the fears we confront today from a pandemic viral invasion—Covid-19, Avian (Bird) Flu, SARS, AIDS, drug resistant viruses, etc. *The Invasion* virus is spread via the exchange of bodily fluids from one infected human to an uninfected one—via spitting and vomiting into their mouths. A few humans are immune from the infection and the aliens see such people as the greatest threat of all. Truly, Jack Finney's story can be interpreted by each subsequent generation and becomes the dominant metaphor of fear for each new decade of viewers.

Inferior to the Siegel and Kaufman versions, *The Invasion* becomes like the finest moments of the original two cinematic versions but features inferior characterizations. Nicole Kidman as the psychiatrist Dr. Bennell is not cleverly drawn and her sidekick Ben Driscoll (a pre-Bond Daniel Craig at his most bland) almost becomes invisible. Veronica Cartwright, the only

holdover from the 1978 version, becomes one of the more interesting characters who contacts Dr. Bennell to complain that her husband is not her husband, and she literally has the task of convincing her doctor that some sort of invasion is at hand. Bennell's "ex" takes her son away for the weekend, and of course the ex-husband is infected and attempts to infect the son (who is immune, even though the viewer watches as his skin becomes scaly as he sleeps, the obvious precursor to the transformation). However, when he awakens, he remains human. When mother comes to fetch her child, she is attacked by the alien threat and infected when her own husband holds her down and spits into her throat, prompting Bennell to invade drug stores for any type of medication that will keep her awake. Walking among the aliens, she must remain emotionless and wide-eyed as she attempts to pass unnoticed.

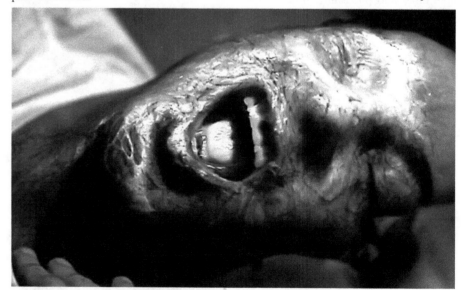

One human being is undergoing the change to an alien.

Perhaps the film's best sequence occurs on a train where Bennell comes across other humans who are also pretending to be aliens, but while Bennell escapes by running down the underground caverns to safety, the aliens overrun the others (one woman can't fake it any longer and screams) and they projectile vomit all over the train car to infect the defenseless humans. The sequence becomes horrifying and visually arresting.

Another segment shines as well—in all these versions we have the scene where Bennell is confronted by a group of aliens who make their pitch that life without emotion would be so much better. Why fight it? Give in and join us in a better life. As the virus spreads, wars are ended, peace accords signed and the hostilities of humanity seem to lessen and almost disappear. When the now alien Driscoll and his cronies make the pitch to Bennell to join them, the aliens have presented their case well—that human beings are violent, war-mongering savages and that the alien virus produces a superior species. However, when Bennell asks about her immune son, the tribe turns things around stating matter of factly that such immune individuals pose the largest threat to the alien consciousness and must be eliminated. It is only this final coda that turns the tide forcing the audience to see the aliens as monstrous, with their speech about eliminating an innocent little boy a horrible thought. But such sloppy script manipulation only attests to the film's flaws. Were it to continue with making its case that the alien society would be superior to our own, that would have produced a thought-provoking and very cerebral movie. But *The Invasion* instead opts for

Nicole Kidman attempts to fit in with the aliens.

Christopher Lee as he appeared in *The Pirates of Blood River*

car chases, explosions, shooting out knee-caps and a happy ending that seems too quick, too easy and too pat.

Unfortunately, while well photographed (in actual Washington and Baltimore location … along with the LA studio lot) with good action sequences and major star power, *The Invasion* becomes only a shadow of the first two versions of Jack Finney's source novel. The alien thesis of theirs being the better world is too quickly truncated, and the almost-too-quick defeating of the virus seems almost as hokey as the ending of *The War of the Worlds*. At least God does not save us here! Despite these flaws, *The Invasion* is a movie best judged by specific sequences and not as a whole. Sometimes even the most mediocre movie features a glimmer of insight and promise.

THE PIRATES OF BLOOD RIVER [2.5]
THE STRANGLERS OF BOMBAY [2.5]
THE DEVIL-SHIP PIRATES [2.5]
THE TERROR OF THE TONGS [3.0]

Most of the Hammer film classics are available on DVD, but several Hammer films fell through the cracks, namely their non-horror output, especially their Eastern murder-cult movies, their pirate films and their war movies. Many fans never saw these less-widely distributed little gems.

Even though the iconic trademark "Hammer Film Productions" is not evident on the cover, the movies presented here are all Hammer films released during the classic era, from the late 1950s through the early 1960s. And while nothing here compares to the early *Dracula* or

Frankenstein films, these Hammer films are nonetheless quite interesting, even though they follow a standard formula, as most B-programmers always do. But the typical Hammer heavyweight personalities (both before and behind the camera) are on clear display and fans who skip watching these films are missing some essential Hammer.

Take, for instance, *The Pirates of Blood River*, a movie shot in HammerScope and color. Because of the limited budget available, this pirate movie is land-based, with a wonderful matte shot of the pirate ship in the background in an opening sequence. But as the title boasts, these pirates wander up the river (most likely not called Blood River) and operate from its

RANSACKING A LOST TROPIC ISLAND... FOR A FABULOUS IDOL OF GOLD!

The Pirates of Blood River

COLOR

KERWIN MATHEWS · GLENN CORBETT · CHRISTOPHER LEE AND MARLA LANDI

Screenplay by JOHN HUNTER and JOHN GILLING From a story by JIMMY SANGSTER Produced by ANTHONY NELSON KEYS
Directed by JOHN GILLING A HAMMER FILM PRODUCTION · A COLUMBIA PICTURES RELEASE

banks. The basic story involves a dashing Jonathan Standish (Kerwin Mathews) exiled to a penal colony for 15 years by his father (a subdued Andrew Keir) for breaking stringent Huguenot law. After suffering indignities and being forced to break rocks on a chain gang, Standish is kidnapped by pirates who force him to take them to his village where they believe a great treasure is located. The pirates are led by another dashing entity, Christopher Lee (who plays LaRoche), whose performance is much more low-key and natural than the usual stiff villains he portrayed at this point in his career (speaking about his human performances, not his monstrous ones). In fact, his affected French accent and line delivery makes LaRoche one of his better performances. Thought truncated, his swordfight with Mathews at the movie's climax is visually exciting and shows Lee to be pretty good with a broadsword. Even though this is not technically a horror film, the gruesome aspects are played up. Sequences of torture, sword piercings and death occur regularly, and a horrific sequence involves people trapped in the river when invading schools of piranha attack, leaving their human victims a bloody pulp.

John Gilling directs and co-writes the screenplay (based upon a Jimmy Sangster story), and his Hammer productions (*The Plague of the Zombies*, *The Reptile*) are always cited as being under-appreciated. Gilling loves to work with perrenial Hammer

Another shot of Christopher Lee from *The Pirates of Blood River*

The "children of Kali" are ready to strangle and kill without spilling a drop of blood.

character actor Michael Ripper, and here Ripper portrays LaRoche's right-hand man, a violent pirate himself (Mack). In this large supporting role, Ripper gets to chew up the scenery playing his pirate as broad (and wonderful) as they come. Mack rates among Ripper's better roles. It is comparable (and similar) to his performance in *Night Creatures*.

And let it be noted that *The Pirates of Blood River*, as are all four features in this collection, have been remastered to pristine video print perfection. Here, the colors are bold, and the digital print is blemish-free with very little annoying grain. The film appears to have been released last year, it's that good.

The Stranglers of Bombay is the only black-and-white feature included, but it too has been rendered in HammerScope and the pristine digital print is sharp with excellent contrast. It is a shame that this Terence Fisher-directed 1959 production was not shot in color, as the military costumes and India locales would look terrific in color. Even though the production was of course filmed at Bray Studios and not Bombay, India, the production design by Bernard Robinson was worthy of the full Technicolor treatment.

Opening with a pounding theme by James Bernard (his entire score is simply wonderful, as usual), *The Stranglers of Bombay* focuses upon the Thuggee cult who worshiped the female God, Kali. In the film's opening moments, the cult's indoctrinator, the High Priest of Kali (George Pastell, who played the Egyptian High Priest in *The Mummy*), speaks to the "children of Kali." He explains how Kali attempted to slay a monster, but every drop of blood spilt grew into another monster, and the viscious cycle continued. Until Kali needed to figure out a method to kill the monster without spilling blood, and thus the cult of strangulation death was born. These young novices are initiated into the cult when their forearm is sliced open with a knife and then immediately branded with a red-hot poker. Typically, such a sequence is a trademark Hammer horror one, and the violence remains dominant throughout. Some of the cult members have infiltrated the powerful British East India Company. The brand on their forearms echoes the similar plot device used earlier in *Enemy from Space* (*Quatermass II*). Guy Rolfe plays the rigid Captain Harry Lewis, insensitive to local customs, whose job it is to discover why caravans are mysteriously vanishing off

the face of the Earth. By the film's end we learn that murderous Thuggees attack en masse and quickly dispatch the entire caravan. The other members of the cult have already dug shallow graves in the desert and the bodies are buried hastily never to be found.

As in most second-tier Hammer productions, the climax descends quickly and the movie ends much too rapidly, but for an 80-minute movie that's generally not a problem. Hammer, bless their hearts, were

proponents of the get in/get out quickly theory of filmmaking. Here, the climax involves one caravan being overrun and slaughtered and the bodies buried efficiently in the desert. In the following sequence, Harry Lewis sneaks through the desert alone and from the underbrush watches as the High Priest incites his cult followers. Lewis manages to get one shot off before he is captured and brought before the High Priest, who is about to burn the bodies of two cultists who died in the mayhem. However, one of the disciples, a young man who the camera lingered on in the opening sequence and throughout the cult sequences, finds Western religion and cuts the rope binding Lewis' hands. The wily captain is then able to throw the High Priest onto the burning funeral pyre, screaming and dying in the most dramatic Hammer death sequence possible. Soon the cult is paralyzed with fear now that their leader is gone and somehow Lewis manages to survive unscathed. However, in the film's coda, he announces that this is only the beginning and that the fight shall continue.

The Devil-Ship Pirates (1964), the second of Hammer's pirate movies, again stars Christopher Lee as Captain Robeles—the villainous captain of the pirate ship. Again, Lee appears youthful, dashing and cruel, but his performance

here is more of what fans expect. Even though he plays a Spaniard, he speaks with his full-throttle English accent. His

A foreign poster for *The Devil-Ship Pirates*

performance is not stiff, nor is it subtle or surprising. In one early sequence, after the Spanish Armada is attacked, most of Robeles' ships are damaged and he needs to get his ship past the British and to shore to make the necessary repairs. One member of the crew sees this as treason and demands the command of the ship be turned over to him. As soon as this blowhard bellows and turns his back, Robeles draws his pistol and, leering, shoots him in the back. The victim still lives, so Robeles orders the man thrown overboard but quickly changes his mind. If he's alive by the next day, he will hang him.

The movie's cast contains many Hammer stock players. Michael Ripper returns as Pepe, one of the pirate crew, and his role here shows promise when he begins to risk the pirates' secrecy by attempting to molest all the village women, but his part is soon relegated to obscurity and inaction. Andrew Keir becomes almost invisible playing a village father of one of the heroes and his usually high energy is woefully absent. Duncan Lamont plays the Bosun with a little spice and the lovely Suzan Farmer looks vulnerable as one of the captured village girls who are taken aboard ship. The male leads Barry Warren and John Cairney are bland at best.

Fortunately, the film opens with some effective model ships of

Christopher Lee disturbs the drinking in a tavern in *The Devil-Ship Pirates*.

the *Diablo* at sea with Robeles and his crew under attack. Unlike *The Pirates of Blood River*, some of the action occurs aboard the Spanish privateer ship. However, when the Spanish Armada falls and the *Diablo* is heavily damaged, the remainder of the film shows the ship docked inland in the process of being repaired. The climax features a fiery explosion aboard the still-moored ship (an actual prop manufactured by Hammer) where it is destroyed.

The plot becomes very talky and involves the Spanish pirates trying to convince the local citizens of the village where the ship was hidden that Spain defeated the British navy and that the Spaniards are the victors and now in charge. Of course, exactly the opposite occurred, but it does not take too long for the villagers to wise up and mount a mutiny to overthrow pirate control.

Christopher Lee's dueling finale using fencing foils is quite exciting, and in another dramatic cinematic opportunity, he also gets to fight with long poles displaying his prowless as Captain Robeles. Unfortu-

nately, his death is less than dynamic when he is shot from afar by a pistol.

The screenplay by Jimmy Sangster is by-the-numbers and the direction by Don Sharp, who directed *Kiss of the Vampire* for Hammer, is lethargic lacking a sense of dramatic pacing. John Gilling did a much better job with his earlier *The Pirates of Blood River*, even without the benefit of onboard pirate ship action.

Although the film may be substandard, its presentation is anything but. Quite simply, the mastering of the print is blemish free and for once the color looks intense and deeply saturated like Technicolor should look. Sequences exist, especially beneath the deck while aboard the pirate ship at the beginning, where the visuals almost take your breath away. The disc is sharp and oozing color—the movie looks pristine and brand new. Too bad the film itself is pesdestrian and quite ordinary.

Without doubt, the gem of this collection is *The Terror of The Tongs*, the closest Hammer came to producing a Fu Manchu–inspired entry. In his initial scene, the perhaps too-tall Lee sits in a chair and appears to be purposely stooping. He portrays the Red Dragon Tong leader Chung King, a mysterious Asian who controls the dockside rackets, as well as controlling the white slavery and drug trade. Even though Lee does not do much more than posture and deliver dialogue, his visual presence commands every sequence in which he appears. Today it is not politically correct for an Occidental to portray an Asian, but the makeup and costumes (aided by a fabulous print and deeply saturated color) are very

impressive, and Lee does a surprisingly effective job.

Jimmy Sangster's screenplay is nicely constructed, and Anthony Bushell, not a typical director for the production company, does a wonderful job in keeping the plot and action developing and the performances crisp. The musical score by Hammer favorite James Bernard is robust and his quiet, quivering strings telegraph when the audience should be afraid.

Perhaps the chief strength of the movie is its expensive look, the production design by Bernard Robinson and the art direction by Thomas Goswell were never better looking. The production, bursting with intensity of color and depth of field, looks far more lavish than it really is. The ornate throne room of Chung King is spacious and sumptuous. But the exterior dock set (an interior set-bound one) is incredible (since it is leftover from another movie). During an early sequence a secret messenger who travels aboard the ship helmed by Captain Sale (Geoffrey Toone) to deliver the names of members of the Red Dragon Tong cult is executed by a rampaging Tong, who rushes at Mr. Ming (Burt Kwouk) with a ceremonial hatchet. Ming pulls his pistol and fires, but the opium-fueled assassin charges to plant his hatchet into Ming's chest, killing him immediately. Unknown by the Tong, Ming has hidden his vital list of names inside a book of poetry he gave Captain Sale to give his 16-year-old daughter, Helena. Just the manner in which the sequence is staged, directed, photographed and edited is superb. The set's depth of field and the high- and low- angle shots only add.

Jimmy Sangster's screenplay is among his best, simply because his story

Milton Reid turns up the torture in *The Terror of The Tongs*.

moves along at a fast clip and features shocking surprises. For instance, after our hero Captain Sale interacts with his innocent and child-like teenage daughter, the audience is shocked when the Tong attack her quarters looking for Ming's list of names. The young girl collapses from shock immediately, but after her room is ransacked and she lies defenseless on her bed, a Tong takes out his knife and stabs the unconscious child to death. Of course, this murder and a father's revenge fuels the plot from this moment on, but a child's death in a Hammer film from that era was shocking. The lovely Yvonne Monlaur (who will always be remembered for her performance as the teacher/heroine in Hammer's *The Brides of Dracula*) submits an equally involving performance here in *The Terror of The Tongs*. She plays a crossbred slave who is sold to a ruthless Tong harbormaster. From her teenage years Lee (Monlaur) had to prepare meals, be a servant and "warm his bed." But when she clunks her master over the head to help Captain Sale, Sale realizes he must protect the beautiful young girl or be responsible for her death at the hands of the Tong. She willingly becomes the servant to the captain and soon confesses her love to him—always with a glint in her eye, purring that she would be willing to warm his bed, but the captain, still grief stricken, is obsessed with revenge and too properly British to take obvious advantage of such a wonderful carnal opportunity. She lovingly nurses him back to health after he is tortured by Chung King's chief torturer. In another surprising plot twist, the captain is informed of an impending Tong assassination attempt on him. He willingly faces his assassin in the hope that the local dockworkers will at last rise up and fight the Red Dragon Tong menace. Chung King offers the assassin a wild night of opium and sex with beautiful women. The killer attacks Sale, however, once again the gun shots from Sale's pistol have little effect on the cutthroat. The beautiful Lee's last-minute embrace of her Captain allows her to take the impact of the hatchet's deadly blow, allowing Sale to kill the Tong. The audience comes to love the kind and self-sacrificing Lee and her savage death is profoundly sad.

The movie's climax finds Captain Sale confronting Chung King at last, and in a typical let's-end-it-quickly finale, Chung King accepts his defeat and has his right-hand man Tong use his knife to end Chung King's life with honor, avoiding the disgrace of a trial and imprisonment. As Chung King asks for forgiveness from his ancient relatives, he falls over dead and the credits come up immediately.

Even when producing non-horror movies, Hammer was still producing violent and blood-curdling adventures that were permeated with horror sequences, torture and sudden, violent death. None of these films compare to the classic Gothics Hammer produced, but each of these movies is worthwhile, featuring pristine prints and marvelous performances (especially by the likes of Christopher Lee and Michael Ripper). *The Terror of The Tongs* is perhaps the only film included that truly impresses, and it is the film that demands further viewing and analysis. And with those lavishly dressed sets photographed in dazzling Eastman color, *The Terror of The Tongs* becomes a visual treat and gripping drama.

30 DAYS OF NIGHT [3.0]

Graphic novels are ever increasingly becoming a major source for stories and bearing a specific look in today's cinema. Of course, genre cinema is most clearly

Christopher Lee as Chung King in *The Terror of The Tongs*

The vampire cult arrives, headed by Marlowe (Danny Houston), and all hell breaks out, from *30 Days of Night*.

The kill from 30 *Days of Night*

embellished by both artists and writers from the arena of graphic novels. *30 Days of Night* is quite an effective horror movie, primarily because of its influences from the comics. In one sequence, as Sheriff Eben Oleson (Josh Harnett) and his estranged wife Stella (Melissa George) are driving down the highway one night, a powerful vampire races towards their police cruiser and with a loud thud jumps on top of the vehicle. In rapid fire editing, the vampire, silohouetted by the light of the moon, becomes an almost feral beast presence, seemingly flailing its arms and legs, attempting to break through the car's roof to get to the food underneath. The way in which this sequence is shot reminds the audience of dynamic panels rendered by comic artists. The entire film has a visual look of a peacefully oblivious town being besieged by evil, defenseless, and unprepared for the bloodshed which follows. In many ways, the look of this cinematic Barrow, Alaska reminds me more than a little of John Carpenter's *The Thing*. True in *The Thing* we do not have a town but a military base, but the frozen emptiness and solitude make the look of both claustrophobic set-pieces the perfect setting for horror.

First the creepy "Stranger" (Ben Foster) arrives and destroys all forms of communications and escape (including a rather grisly death of all the town's sled dogs). Then the vampire cult arrives, led by Marlowe (Danny Houston, John's son), who gives vampire cinema an entirely new look. Marlowe, almost always without emotion, keeps his black-

ened eyes wide open. Even though, as stated, these vampires can move rapidly, Marlowe is most creepy when he moves deliberately slow. His bloodied face and hair, his elongated fingernails smeared with blood, sometimes make him seem subordinate to his cult. Most of these other vampires have prosthetic faces and look like horror movie vampire monsters. But Marlowe, either young or old, always seems to have the expression of a scientist looking through a microscope at a specimen on a glass slide. In his slow-glide manner, he is the other-species fiend who is investigating the inferior humans on whom he will feed. And after staring, circling and all so lightly touching his terrified victim, he will, with sudden force, use his fingernails to slash the face and neck of his victims, before plunging downward for the kill. He only speaks in an ancient, European language, frequently translated as subtitles, but its not his voice that matters, but his full body expression. Cinema has never created his type of vampire before now (forget his makeup effect cronies) and Danny Houston submits a finely crafted persona of evil. Too bad his quick death is unworthy of the performance.

What makes *30 Days of Night* rise above most of the other modern horror movies is the attention paid to the characterization of all the major townies we encounter, both straight-lace and warped (we are reminded that people live their life of isolation in Barrow because of the sense of wilderness and freedom; these

aren't the typical United States citizens). It is precisely because of the introduction and conflict that exists between all these locals that makes us care when the vampires, at first only seen by rustling sounds and quickly moving shadows, come in for the kill. Far too many modern horror movies throw casts of characters at the audience that are seldom defined, let alone developed. Or if their characters are explored, these people are almost as horrible and unlikable as the monsters that threaten them. Here, in *30 Days of Night*, we observe broken people trying to heal broken relationships, we see the bond of love among families, we see the craziness of friendship, we see the ultimate sacrifice, self sacrifice. And into this isolated world of *30 days of Night*, we encounter the invading vampire cult that can kill at will.

Director David Slade, whose other film *Hard Candy* garnered critical attention a few years ago, demonstrates a strong visual style. Yes, he does trip over a few unwise artistic choices (the stereotypical, monstrous vampires whose blood-caked faces and poses substitute for performances, among others), and the climax and ending are unsatisfying. Just like the climax of John Carpenter's *The Thing*, the entire environment goes up in flames, but the final duel between hero and villain is woefully unsatisfying, even though the very final sequence, watching the sun rise once again, is a perfect touch. Flawed yet inspired, *30 Days of Night* creates something innovative and new for the anemic-vampire cinema.

ALIEN [5.0]
ALIENS [5.0]

We want to make this one short and sweet. Over 40 years after the fact, *Alien*, Ridley Scott's 1979 horror film classic, stands as one of the greats of the horror film genre, a movie that merges the horror and science fiction film genre. As far as being a monster film, it presents one of filmdom's originals, an alien that goes out of its way to not resemble a man in a rubber suit. With its elongated head and slithery upside-down movement, Scott makes this creature move in non-human ways. And once human victims are frozen in terror, the jaws-within-jaws spring forth, taking another life. The photography by Derek Vanlint is wondrous, making an unglamorous space vessel look drippy, dank, unpleasant, drab and dark. His pans upward or from side-to-side accent the haunted Halloween feel of the vessel and the quiet musical score and ambient sounds of footsteps or water dripping only heighten the terror. When Dallas (Tom Sherritt) roams the claustrophobic air ducts to only see a split-second flash of the alien above him, as frantic nervous Nelly Lambert (Veronica Cartwright)

The Face Hugger from *Alien*

watches the alien approach Dallas on her tracking screen, screaming for him to get out immediately, the scene becomes one of the film's pivotal scares. The slow Val Lewton-esque walk by hang-dog Brett (Harry Dean Stanton), as he looks for Jones the cat, is another classic scene. The feline recoils in terror at the approaching alien presence, Brett remaining oblivious, even as the creature's tail uncoils unseen behind him, the camera is focused on the terrified cat's eyes. Even the alien birth sequence, exploding out of Kane's stomach (John Hurt) as it scampers away, remains terrifying to this day. As is the initial sequence on the alien planet where Kane first examines one of the eggs and finds a face hugger burst through the membrane and attach itself to his face and neck. Whether the scares are slow building or intense jump shots, the effect is masterful and terrifying, always accented with expert photography and subtle editing.

The performances are workmanlike but represent good ensemble acting. But the then unknown Sigourney Weaver as Ripley steals the show. Her immediate likeability dominated by her careful observance of the rules and a hardboiled commitment to following them, even if it means the sacrifice of one individual, is commendable. Even when the entire crew rises up to challenge her ideas, Lambert even bitch-slapping her in anger and frustration, Ripley knows what must be done to survive. Even if that means when attempting to enter a hibernation chamber while wearing skimpy underwear, she must battle the alien one final time. She never makes an unwise move, and her ex-

pressions of terror are equaled by her quiet determination of survival at any cost. Ripley becomes an iconic female Beowulf for a new generation of moviegoers, a template riptide for ass-kicking heroines during the following decade. But Weaver's performance is based upon registering intense fear at the same moments she is plotting her own survival. The blending of utter terror and utter control makes her Ripley an iconic hero.

In 1979, at age 29, *Alien* scared the living hell out of pal Wayne Shipley and me at the Uptown Theater in Washington, DC. It is a cinematic experience I will never forget, and the film has lost none of its bite in the decades since. On 4k disc the film has never looked or sounded better since that Uptown show palace experience. It remains one of the most artistic and terrifying movies of all time.

Aliens is an anomaly; it's the sequel that rivals the quality of the original. I still feel that Ridley Scott's *Alien* is the superior film, perhaps by a nose, merely because the mythology, biology and look of the monstrous aliens were created in that 1979 original. But James Cameron's faithful sequel is also spectacular, remaining one of the best horror movies ever produced.

In *Aliens*, the supporting ensemble crew might be even better than the one in the original (which was excellent) and the character development, especially of Ripley (Sigourney Weaver) and her bond with the orphaned child Newt (Carrie Henn), is superior. Here Ripley is again a kick-butt heroine, but she is shown to be psychologically scared and scarred. She has been drifting in space for 57 years, discovering that her 11-year-old daughter has died three years ago, childless, at age 66. So, when the lone survivor of the human base on the alien planet turns out to be

Sigourney Weaver as Ripley from *Alien*

Newt, around 11 years old, we all know that Ripley's mission will be to replace the loss of one child with the redemption of saving another. And Newt is a pint-sized version of Ripley, a survivor who thinks before she acts. Lightweight comedian Paul Reiser becomes the perfect choice for the "company's" face, the caring and concerned corporate manager who turns out to be evil through and through, even going so far as to trap Newt and Ripley in a sealed laboratory with two face huggers hoping to impregnate one or both of them so that he can slip one of the creatures back to Earth and the corporation. He submits the performance of his career, and it is a very effective one.

The ensemble cast is wonderful, framed by the three major characters: Hicks (Cameron's go-to hero Michael Biehn), Hudson (Bill Paxton), Vasquez (Jenette Goldstein) and synthetic Bishop (Lance Henriksen). Ripley, based upon her experiences from the first movie, hates and is fearful of all synthetics, but Bishop appears committed and faithful, and he gradually earns Ripley's respect.

The wonderful Bill Paxton plays cowardly Hudson who over-reacts, becomes too emotional and screams out the oft quoted line that will always be remembered,

"Game over! Game over!" However, during the final barrage where he is attacked by an alien who appears from beneath the metal grill he stands on, Hudson dies a courageous death giving the alien army more than they ever bargained for, redeeming himself by his actions. Besides

The full cast of *Aliens*

providing comic relief and spunk, Paxton's performance shifts from over-cocky to fearful, to cowardly, to self-sacrificing and brave; he does a nice job. Jenette Goldstein as Vasquez becomes the steroid female warrior that would be overkill for Ripley. While Ripley is feminine and courageous, Vasquez becomes more of a man than Hudson could ever wish to be. Yes, she is a stereotype but her humanity and skill as a warrior endears her character to audiences. Michael Biehn contains the right amount of romance and action, and he becomes the perfect foil for Ripley, especially in the sequence where he teaches her how to fire his massive weapon, with Ripley fondling every inch of the cold steel and stating proudly, "I know how to handle myself." And in this performance, Lance Henriksen remains calm and reserved, demonstrating intelligence and courage when needed, but perhaps he is remembered for his "Not bad for a human" line, delivered as his body has been cut in half after Ripley has

banished the alien queen into outer space forever.

While *Alien* is a true horror movie that just happens to occur in outer space and on an alien planet, *Aliens* is a war movie emphasizing the military regiment camaraderie and bravery in battle. In other words, *Aliens* is more the action movie while *Alien* is more the haunted house spook feast. So, both films approach their subject matter from different perspectives, each totally successful. If one were to find one criticism of *Aliens*, it might be in the theory that one alien is better than 20. In *Alien* Ridley Scott went out of his way to photograph the creature from awkward angles, often showing the creature curled up upside-down or awkwardly fitting into a tight space. He uses his camera to show the utter other worldliness of the creature and the monster always appears totally unique and terrifying. In Cameron's *Aliens*, we have many alien drones, and none have the finesse of the lone creature from the first film. The creature's face and jaws do not seem quite as lifelike or real. Not even the alien queen seems as majestically created as she moves awkwardly,

and her facial features are never as minutely defined as the alien in the original production. Also, when we see the alien drones getting blown to smithereens, we have a quick flash of a body part fly into the air or

a flash of a brightly lit face. But we never dwell on the majesty of the creature in the same loving way that Scott revealed his creature in *Alien*. In this case, more is necessary to the story, but as far as visuals and horror goes, *Alien*'s single monstrous entity remains more terrifying than the army of monsters that appear in *Aliens*.

(top) Ripley attempts to save Newt (Carrie Henn) from the alien monster; (middle) The alien sneaks up on Newt, dragging her under water.

FINAL MUTTERINGS

BY GARY J. SVEHLA

Funny how things happen. Issue #81, this current issue, was supposed to be the final one, to go out after 59 years of publication. But to me a 60th anniversary issue sounds sweet and who wants to exit after only 59 years of publication?

So, we are gearing up for issue #82, and have already announced articles are due **January 15, 2023**. If you are a newbie or a veteran, we want your articles. If you feel more secure, we can discuss article ideas via e-mail (e-mail address available on the first page.)

It must be the ending of an era as editor/publisher Dick Klemensen and Nancy have announced the end of his publication when he turns 78 and publishes his 51st issue (he published a double-issue that counted as two issues), so that makes 50 issues in 50 years. If you are fans of British horror movies and love Klemensen's magazine, you may also wish there was a counterpart to the classic Universal horror classics on Klemensen's level of expertise being published, or simply consider *Little Shoppe of Horrors* to be among the best genre magazines ever published, simply said, and done. Because of the quality,

it will be very hard to say good-bye. But we all wear an explanation tag and slow down with time. *Little Shoppe of Horror* represents a pinnacle of quality and will be sorely missed.

Now on to the major decision we will have to make … will the 4k of *Invaders from Mars* be worth $70 for a one-disc set where the movie runs a mere 75 minutes (included with a commemorative poster autographed by star Jimmy Hunt), limited to 1,000 copies? Making the decision easier, restoration master Scott Mac-Queen says a more mainstream copy will be available later at a "lower price point." But are you willing to pay $70 for a one-disc movie with an autographed poster *today*? Film Detective shook up the apple cart when the Film Noir Foundation released several restored and rare noir titles for around a market price of $40 each, but $70? Well, Jan Willem of Ignite Films (he comes from the Netherlands) personally paid for the total cost of restoration of *Invaders from Mars* himself and he probably wants his money back at last. But you must consider, the home disc market is rapidly moving from

the mainstream and becoming a niche product, which will eventually sell for more since fewer copies of physical media will be sold. The trend is to stream movies and not to own tangible media. But readers of this magazine all know the collector's market and understand the demand to own something that you can actually hold in your hands. But if we pay the higher price for the Collector's Edition of *Invaders from Mars* today, how long will it be before more and more Blu ray/4k disks all start costing around $70 or more? Or physical media that used to cost $20 a pop now might cost more than three times that. But again, Scott MacQueen promises a mainstream edition at a much lower cost. Anyway, we thank him for recent restored editions of *Doctor X*, *Mystery of the Wax Museum*, *The Vampire Bat*, *White Zombie*, *The Phantom of The Monastery*, *The Devil and Daniel Webster* and many others during the past 10 years at UCLA Film Preservation. We wish him the best in his retirement.

Anyway, be on the lookout for issue #82 of *Midnight Marquee* sometime in 2023.

CPSIA information can be obtained
at www.ICGtesting.com
Printed in the USA
LVHW051027221122
733767LV00007B/79